This book helped me rethink our family's plans for next week and for next year. If you feel like your stress, busyness, and distraction are sapping healthy rhythms from your life, Glenn and Holly Packiam are welcome and practical guides. You won't feel like you are reading about something ideal but unattainable. This is a book for real people, and the steps shown here can lead us to better lives.

> RUSSELL MOORE, public theologian at *Christianity Today* and director of *Christianity Today*'s Public Theology Project

The best part of this book is that a wife and husband are literally on the same page, in pursuit of God-honoring intentionality in their personal, marriage, family, and ministry lives. I love how Glenn and Holly weave their personal story into their desire for abundantly intentional years together. A richly spiritual, warmly relational, and vibrantly practical resource.

> STEPHEN A. MACCHIA, founder and president of Leadership Transformations, director of the Pierce Center for Disciple-Building at Gordon-Conwell Theological Seminary, and author of *The Discerning Life*

Glenn and Holly Packiam have crafted a book that's about so much more than just setting goals—they're showing us God's invitation to abundance through living with intentionality toward Jesus. What does it mean to create rhythms of renewal, rest, and refreshment in this hurried day and age? The Packiams answer that question beautifully with pastoral guidance and practical wisdom.

> AUBREY SAMPSON, pastor, speaker, and author of *Known*

The breakneck pace of life in the modern world is leaving many of us exhausted and at a loss. In *The Intentional Year*, Glenn and Holly Packiam invite us to take a deep breath and settle ourselves amid the mad rush of a culture moving with far too much speed and far too little intention. Pastorally warm, theologically rich, and practically accessible, this book is a wonderful guide down a new path, toward the freedom, peace, and purpose every human truly longs for.

JAY Y. KIM, pastor of Westgate Church and author of *Analog Christian*

What a beautiful and life-giving book from Glenn and Holly. Together they have cultivated a life of purpose and significance through their intentional practices, and now they've invited us to make those our own. Our intentions embody our values. Whether you're an expert at intentions or are just starting down the path, Glenn and Holly have invited us into rhythms that are both simple and profound.

TRICIA LOTT WILLIFORD, author of *This Book Is for You* and *You Can Do This*

Our world is full of chaos and disorder, but our daily lives can be different. Glenn and Holly have lived intentional lives, full of healthy habits and rhythms, and now we get to glean from their years of learning. You will find strength, wisdom, and encouragement on each of these pages.

BRADY BOYD, senior pastor of New Life Church and author of *Addicted to Busy*

We live in a busy world in which too many of us don't take the time to stop and reflect on what is happening in our lives, our families, and our world. This often results in stress, anxiety, and burnout. One of the ways we can guard our souls from spiritual burnout is by rediscovering the ancient rhythms of grace that are deeply rooted in the historic Christian faith. In *The Intentional Year*, Glenn and Holly Packiam invite us to slow down, take an inventory of our lives, and cultivate daily rhythms of prayer, rest, renewal, and work. This book provides a road map for how we can develop spiritual rhythms that have the power to transform us from the inside out and make us increasingly like Jesus Christ.

DR. WINFIELD BEVINS, author of *Liturgical Mission*

When my wife, Rochelle, and I started taking three days at the end of every year to reflect, celebrate, and plan, it took our relationship with each other—and with God—to another level. Even at that, *The Intentional Year* takes it another step forward. Glenn and Holly unpack how to use and leverage your and your partner's gifts and callings to bring light and goodness to a world immersed in darkness. Every couple needs that. You can't imagine how you will be blessed.

SEAN ISAAC PALMER, author of *Speaking by the Numbers*

THE INTENTIONAL YEAR

simple rhythms for finding
freedom, peace, and purpose

HOLLY + GLENN PACKIAM

A NavPress resource published in alliance
with Tyndale House Publishers

NavPress is the publishing ministry of The Navigators, an international Christian organization and leader in personal spiritual development. NavPress is committed to helping people grow spiritually and enjoy lives of meaning and hope through personal and group resources that are biblically rooted, culturally relevant, and highly practical.

For more information, visit NavPress.com.

The Intentional Year: Simple Rhythms for Finding Freedom, Peace, and Purpose

Copyright © 2022 by Glenn Packiam and Holly Packiam. All rights reserved.

A NavPress resource published in alliance with Tyndale House Publishers

NavPress and the NavPress logo are registered trademarks of NavPress, The Navigators, Colorado Springs, CO. *Tyndale* is a registered trademark of Tyndale House Ministries. Absence of ® in connection with marks of NavPress or other parties does not indicate an absence of registration of those marks.

The Team: David Zimmerman, Publisher; Caitlyn Carlson, Acquisitions Editor; Jennifer Lonas, Copy Editor; Olivia Eldredge, Operations Manager; Julie Chen, Designer; Sarah K. Johnson, Proofreader

Cover illustration of color grid by Julie Chen. Copyright © 2022 by Tyndale House Ministries. All rights reserved.

Author photo by Ashlee Weaver, copyright © 2022. All rights reserved.

Published in association with The Bindery Agency, www.TheBinderyAgency.com

Some of the anecdotal illustrations in this book are true to life and are included with the permission of the persons involved. All other illustrations are composites of real situations, and any resemblance to people living or dead is purely coincidental.

For information about special discounts for bulk purchases, please contact Tyndale House Publishers at csresponse@tyndale.com, or call 1-855-277-9400.

ISBN 978-1-64158-394-7

Printed in the United States of America

28	27	26	25	24	23	22
7	6	5	4	3	2	1

To our parents, Bill and Roxanne and David and Karmen,
for all the big and small ways you intentionally love us.

CONTENTS

FOREWORD

Have you ever thought, *I need a plan—a good, simple plan to deepen my faith.*

If that has ever crossed your mind, you are among the millions of people who have thought the same thing but haven't been shown a way to do this. How do we grow in our lives with God? How can we better integrate our faith into the mundane ordinariness of life? How can our faith form in us the kind of character we truly long for? How can we live with a heightened sense of God's presence?

As a pastor, I'm regularly in conversation with people asking these questions—people who want a faith that matters, a faith for one's entire life and not just for the overtly spiritual moments of a given year. But cultivating this kind of faith can feel daunting. "Where do I begin?" "What should I focus on?" "Is there a simple way to begin the journey (or to deepen what I've already been doing)?" These are the questions I'm often asked. Frankly, these are the questions I'm thinking about *for myself* on a regular basis.

When it comes to growing in our lives with God, ourselves, and others, we need more than religious platitudes and spiritual hype—we need trusted guides who can take our hand and show us the way. And I thank God for this book you're holding because I can't think of better guides to lead you into a more intentional faith life.

I've known Glenn and Holly Packiam for a number of years. We have shared many a meal together. We have spent numerous hours in conversation about faith and life. In the years I've known them, I've been inspired by the depth of love they share and the breadth of insight they carry. As you will soon read in this book, Holly and Glenn have cultivated an intentional annual rhythm for many years that has established a strong foundation for their marriage. But you need to know something before you turn this page: *This is not simply a book for marrieds.* This is a book for *everyone*, at all stages of faith.

As I read through this book, I was blown away by how much ground they cover in such little space. This is a book you can read rather quickly, and at the same time, it's a book that you will want to return to for years to come. Glenn and Holly offer beautiful theology, accessible spiritual practices, and a refreshing honesty that will put you at ease. Instead of wanting to "try harder," you'll walk away with a longing to order your life in a way that bears good fruit.

The life God has for you far exceeds anything you can imagine, but here's the thing: *It won't happen without intentionality.* You can't autopilot yourself into transformation. The life you long for won't emerge by accident. You need a plan. And I can't think of a better place to start than here.

Rich Villodas
lead pastor of New Life Fellowship
author of The Deeply Formed Life *and* Good and Beautiful and Kind

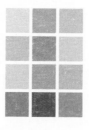

CHAPTER 1

THE SPIRITUALITY OF INTENTIONALITY

Life is what happens . . . while you're busy making other plans.

John Lennon, "Beautiful Boy (Darling Boy)"

GLENN

We should never have met—a farm girl from Iowa and a pastor's kid from Malaysia. Yet there we were, standing outside the classroom building on the campus of Oral Roberts University in Tulsa, Oklahoma.

Some mutual friends introduced us. I was a junior; Holly was a freshman. When we met, neither of us thought much of it. Well, I thought Holly was gorgeous but way out of my league. And thanks to American-TV stereotypes, I concluded from her blonde highlights and tan skin that she was a cheer-leader from California. She, I can only guess, must have looked at me—with my closely cropped hair, gold-rimmed glasses, and argyle-before-argyle-was-cool-again sweater—and thought I was a sweet, nerdy foreign student. (I was wrong about her. She would not have been far off the mark about me!) But here we are, some twenty years into marriage, grateful for the providence of God in guiding us to each other.

Providence, though, is a funny word. Some people use *providence* as a synonym for *fate*, a destiny written in the stars. Christians usually think of providence as the sovereignty of God, who is working in the midst of all things for our good and his glory. But even then, there are questions about where our own choices come in.

The interplay between God's sovereignty and our free will is far too big a conversation for this book, but our marriage is itself a demonstration of the mystery: God drew Holly and me together, and yet he invited our participation. Or to say it another way: God's providence does not preclude our participation. Just because God is involved doesn't make the events of our lives automatic. Somehow . . . somehow . . . God makes room for our action.

HOLLY

My father is a farmer. That's not to say I learned much about farming. My parents had two daughters, and they didn't hold any illusions of our being ranch hands. Still, you don't grow up on 180 acres of corn and alfalfa, with dozens and dozens of beef cattle roaming around, without picking up a few things.

If there's one thing any farmer knows, it's that stuff doesn't grow on its own. Well, let me rephrase that: *Some* stuff grows on its own—just not the stuff you want. Weeds run amok with little human aid. But to grow the crops you want, you've got to be intentional. You have to have a plan. And a rhythm. Even in Iowa, where the soil is rich and fertile. There are things my father did every single spring, things he did every single summer, things he did every single fall, and things he did every single winter. You can't hope for a good harvest in the fall if you wasted time in the spring.

Cultivating fruit may be slow, but it requires intentionality. My farming father once told Glenn that he had to farm slowly on purpose. "Every magazine I read tells me how *not* progressive I am, and how that's a bad thing," Dad said. "I have to be *intentionally regressive*. For me, farming is a way of life. I think of farming as a vocation."

Farming is a wonderful picture of the human vocation, the calling to be a human being. When God made the first man and woman, he placed them in a garden and gave them charge over it. Having been made in his image, they were to reflect his wise and loving order in the world. They were to bring order out of chaos and fruitfulness out of potential. There, at the beginning of the world, before sin and sickness and evil had begun to infect everything, human beings were called to be cultivators of creation.

Cultivation requires intentionality. Fruitfulness flows from faithfulness. Growth happens only on purpose.

STOPPING ON PURPOSE

When a blizzard hits where we live in Colorado, everything stops. No school. No meetings. No soccer practice or dance class or music lessons. Everything just stops. Yet most of us never stop. With Zoom and Teams and everything else online these days, even a blizzard can't make us stop.

But this book is an invitation to stop. To listen. To pray. To be free of stress and anxiety and worry. To live intentionally.

The trouble is, life happens *to* us. The alarm goes off, and we stumble out of bed and begin our day, moving from one appointment to the next, mindlessly scrolling social media during the lulls between things. By the time we get home, our brains are fried and our souls are depleted, but our bodies just keep moving on autopilot. Prepare dinner, clean up the kitchen, take the dog for a walk, get the kids to bed, scroll social media again.

How do we get off this train?

We don't have time to step back from our days, much less from our lives, to examine what we're doing and why, right? Or so we think.

The frantic pace we find ourselves struggling to keep doesn't have to be our reality. We can live with a sense of vision, purpose, and deliberateness that helps us order our days.

It may be helpful to think of your life in a few specific

spheres. We can live more intentionally when we name those spheres. It may be that we already devote time and energy to those places, those dimensions of our lives. Or it may be that in naming these spheres, we recognize that we are not devoting the time and energy we should to those places. In this book, we're going to focus on five key spheres—prayer, rest, renewal, relationships, and work—that require our attention and investment if we want to live a more purposeful and abundant life.

Then, we must choose to interrupt the cycle of default living by *stopping intentionally* to examine *how* we want to live within these spheres of our lives. This can unfold in different ways depending on the person, but we'd recommend marking out a couple of times a year to get away, pray, reflect, and plan for the season ahead.

A little over a decade ago, Glenn and I began talking with several couples who prioritized going on an annual or semi-annual retreat to reflect on the previous year and look ahead to the coming year. The couples went to different places and followed different rhythms during their retreats, but their intentionality was the same. We noticed these couples were *choosing* to orient their lives around God. This kind of lifestyle didn't just automatically fall into place; they purposefully carved out time every year to pay attention to what God was doing in their lives and look ahead to where they were going.

We were inspired to follow in their footsteps, and so we embarked on our first retreat. We ventured to a historic site in our community that rented affordable rooms and provided breakfast. Being in a place where breakfast was provided felt like a small luxury for parents of three little ones! We spent two nights away from home, taking time to rest, delight in the Lord and each other, reflect on the past year, and prayerfully discern what God might have for us in the coming year.

For a dozen years or so, Glenn and I have been carving out time for our annual retreat at the end of December or the beginning of January. Our retreat plan has ebbed and flowed during this time, but in recent years we've come up with a rhythm to guide us into a more intentional life. Here's what our retreat rhythm usually looks like:

- **Connect, share, and process:** For the first night of our retreat, we enjoy an evening out just to catch our breath and share our hearts with each other. Processing helps us shift our focus to rest and reflection from the chaos of normal life, with carpool driving, meal prep, work, parties—you get the idea. If you're single, an evening out might include treating yourself to an amazing meal or going to one of your favorite spots. It could also be fun to invite two or three trusted friends to join you on a retreat.

- **Reflect on the past and on what lies ahead:** The next morning, we each find a private spot to journal and pray reflectively about the previous year (or six months if we do this twice a year). We look back at the goodness of God and name the grief and gifts of the past season. Then we take time to look ahead and listen for God's direction. Is there a key word or theme we need to pay attention to, a sort of framing story for the season to come?

- **Connect, share, and process:** After a time of individual reflection and listening to God, we come together over lunch and process what God has shown us. We share from our journals and talk about any key words or themes we received fom God regarding the months ahead.

- **Take an inventory of five spheres of life:** We spend the rest of the afternoon reflecting on the spheres of prayer, rest, renewal, relationships, and work and the rhythms that have characterized our lives in each of these spheres over the past year. What rhythms have helped us connect with God, stop and reflect, rest and renew? Which rhythms do we want to continue in the coming year? Are there any new practices we could start? What relationships have we invested in over the past year? Are there people we want to bring in close in the coming months, or relationships we need to let go of for a time? Finally, we evaluate the work we're doing—paid or unpaid—and ask the Lord to help us see if anything needs to change. Maybe the work doesn't align with the gifts God has given us, the growth we've experienced, or the capacity we actually have in this season.

- **Connect, share, and process:** Over dinner in the evening, we discuss our inventory of practices, comparing notes and finding places of unity. Sharing and processing helps us shape a vision for the coming year.

- **Establish rhythms for the next season:** The final morning, we bring together everything we've been talking about and establish rhythms for each sphere of life in the coming year. What specific practices do we want to engage in that will help us pray, rest, be renewed, connect in relationships, and work?

- **Make a plan of action:** After a break for lunch, we do the unglamorous but crucial work of turning our list of practices for the next season of our lives into dates and times on the calendar. When will we go on dates? When will we set aside time for rest and renewal? When will we pray or work out or have friends over? If the practices we've established don't make it onto our calendar and become scheduled events, they will remain abstract ideas.

This rhythm for our annual retreats has anchored our marriage and household for more than a decade. It has become our garden box for fruitfulness, the trellis for our life on the vine.

Even if you don't start off a new season with an annual retreat, incorporating key practices at different points during the year can be a game changer. In the following chapters, we'll walk you through rhythms that reflect the five spheres of life. These rhythms, or sets of practices, will help you find freedom from anxiety and hurry and transition from auto-pilot mode to purposeful living.

First, let's talk about the importance of practice.

THE POWER OF PRACTICE

There was a brief time when I held the record at my small high school for the most three-pointers in a game: seven. It didn't last long, but it was fun while it did!

Basketball is a sport of streaks. Players can go on a tear, making every shot they heave up, and then they can go cold, throwing nothing but bricks. When a hot streak ends, even the best shooters can't seem to make a bucket. In basketball, as in many other sports, athletes can't control the outcome of a game or even their own performance. But they can control their *preparation*. That's why so many athletes set goals around practice routines rather than performance outcomes. For a basketball player, that may mean setting a goal of shooting one hundred three-pointers before and after every practice, as opposed to trying to become a 40 percent three-point shooter over the course of a season. Players never know what their shooting percentage will be, but they can decide what their practice routine will look like.

Not everyone values practice the same way, however. Glenn likes to recall a press conference in 2002 when reporters were interrogating a young NBA star named Allen Iverson for not practicing with his team, the Philadelphia 76ers. Frustrated by the questions, Iverson replied, "If I can't practice, I can't practice. If I'm hurt, I'm hurt. I mean, it's as simple as that." Then he went on a legendary tirade about being grilled for missing practice time:

> It's easy to sum it up when we just talk about practice. We're sitting here . . . I'm supposed to be the franchise player, and we're in here talking about practice. I mean, listen, we're talking about practice. Not a game. Not a game. Not a game. We're talking about practice. Not a game. Not the game that I go out there and die for and play every game like it's my last. Not the game. We're talking about practice, man. I mean how silly is that. And we're talking about practice. I know I'm supposed to be there. I know I'm supposed to lead by example. I know that and I'm not shoving it aside, you know, like it don't mean anything. I know it's important. I do, I honestly do. But we're talking about practice, man. What are we talking about? Practice? We're talking about practice, man? We're talking about practice. We're talking about practice. We ain't talking about the game. We're talking about practice, man.[1]

In the span of just a few minutes, Iverson used the word *practice* fourteen times! This quote became infamous because everyone knows that *practice* is the foundation of *performance*—and dismissing practice means throwing away the long-term goal of enhancing performance on the court. The star player's rant sounded as if he wanted to work hard only when the arena lights were on. That wasn't an accurate read of Iverson's intentions, but you can see why his rant made headlines.

The importance of practice doesn't just apply to basketball. The apostle Paul told young Timothy that living an exemplary Christian life was going to take some work:

> Train yourself for a holy life! While physical training has some value, training in holy living is useful for everything. It has promise for this life now and the life to come. . . . Don't neglect the spiritual gift in you that was given through prophecy when the elders laid hands on you. Practice these things, and live by them so that your progress will be visible to all. Focus on working on your own development and on what you teach. If you do this, you will save yourself and those who hear you.
>
> 1 TIMOTHY 4:7-8, 14-16

The Christian life takes practice. Paul admonishes us to develop lifelong, Spirit-powered practices. Practices are powerful for many reasons. Here are three.

Practices Can Be Catalysts for Change

In *The Power of Habit*, business writer Charles Duhigg writes about the transformative impact of "keystone habits."[2] When people adopt certain habits—from making the bed each morning to making a to-do list every night for the next day—other things in their lives begin to change for the better. A constellation of good habits clusters around one key new habit.

In this book we're going to unpack one new keystone habit: *taking time to stop for the purpose of moving forward.* We'll also discuss the implications of making this habit, or rhythm, an essential part of our lives. We believe that the practices we'll explore in this book can be catalysts for changing the ways we approach our prayer lives, our rest, our renewal, our relationships, and our work. It's a way of interrupting our default mode, our grinding monotony, so we can rediscover purpose, peace, and freedom. The keystone habit of stopping at least once a year to reflect, pray, and plan leads to establishing a set of practices, or rhythms, that will help us become fully alive to the Lord and the people in our lives.

You may not think that sounds spiritual enough. *Why can't God just bring about the changes in our lives that he wants? Why can't we just trust his timing and be content and not stress out so much about spiritual growth?* We tend to believe that God inserts himself into our world like a parent on the sidelines of a toddler soccer game who can only take so much before sprinting onto the field to help the kids know where to go.

But that isn't actually how God works. He isn't waiting for the right moment to intervene, nudging things here and there as needed. He is *already* involved in his world. God created the universe like a composer writing a symphony—and I think he often sings along with the angels, "The whole earth is full of his glory!" (Isaiah 6:3, ESV).

Part of the point of spiritual formation is training our eyes to see and our ears to hear God in the world, and learning to sing along with creation. That requires changing our tune. We can't join in God's symphony if we're singing our own songs. To hear his song, we must begin with silence and tune our hearts to the notes. As we do, we find ourselves increasingly aligning with the work of God.

Practices Prepare Us for Moments of Testing

When we lean into practices, we develop the character required to persevere in moments of testing. Habits are like root systems that run deep underground, connecting us to the Source of living water and preparing us to bear fruit. Or as many spiritual writers have suggested, habits are like a trellis that supports the sometimes-weak vines of our intentions so that fruit can grow in our lives. Habits prepare us for crisis. They help us endure seasons of drought and rise up even when our strength is waning. Habits give substance and direction to our best intentions.

On January 15, 2009, US Airways flight 1549 made an unpowered emergency water landing in the Hudson River after an encounter with a flock of geese caused both jet engines to fail. All 155 passengers and crew aboard successfully evacuated. The incident came to be known as the Miracle on the Hudson. New Testament scholar N. T. Wright uses this illustration to make a point about character, or the "power of right habits."[3] We tend to think that God overrode the course of events that day and miraculously guided the plane to safety. But what if he was working *through* people instead?

After all, the captain of that flight—Chesley "Sully" Sullenberger III—had been flying since he was sixteen. In 1969, Sully enrolled as a student at the United States Air Force Academy, which happens to be located in our city of Colorado Springs. As a freshman, he was one of twelve selected for a glider program. A year later, he became a glider instructor. After graduating from the academy, Sully went to Purdue University for postgraduate studies. Then he served in the Air Force as a fighter pilot for five years, earning the rank of captain. He became a commercial pilot in 1980 and was almost fifty-eight when he landed flight 1549 in the Hudson. He had been flying airplanes for more than forty years! Sully, as Wright points out, was neither relying on spontaneous virtue nor consulting a rule book. He had spent years developing the character and skills required to handle the situation. A lifetime of practice equipped him to land an engineless plane and remain calm in a crisis.

Practices Embed Knowledge

GLENN

Several years ago, when we were visiting Holly's parents on their farm outside Akron, Iowa, one of our children came down with a fever, and we needed some medicine for her. I offered to run to the drugstore in town, just a few miles down the road. I could picture the street in my mind, but I'm more of a word guy, and my sense of direction is pretty bad. (Holly could tell you some stories!) Before heading out the door, I asked what street the store was on. "Main Street," Holly said.

Wanting to double-check, especially since Holly hadn't lived there for several years, I asked her mom, Roxanne.

"It's right on Main Street, Glenn," she said, looking somewhat bewildered.

GPS on phones wasn't quite a thing yet, but how hard could it be to find Main Street in a town with about one thousand people and only one blinking light? So off I went down the road. In short order, I saw a street sign that said "Main Street." I confidently made the turn, only to discover a row of houses. No stores, no bank, no library, no pharmacy. I drove around a bit longer, allowing for the possibility that the town had changed since I had last been there. But it didn't take long to realize that the drugstore was clearly *not* on Main Street. When I finally found the row of businesses—the only row in town—I looked at the street sign. It said "Reed Street."

When I got back to the farmhouse, I promptly informed my wife and mother-in-law that the drugstore was not, in fact, on Main Street but rather on Reed Street.

"Of course," they said, cocking their heads and drawing their breath slowly in an "Ah, yes" sort of way. To them it *was* Main Street no matter what the street signs said.

Holly learned her hometown not from maps or street signs but from riding around with her parents and grandparents. She had ridden her bike on those streets and learned to drive a car through that small, quintessential American town. Her first job was at the drive-in around the corner from "Main Street," and she'd spent summers lifeguarding at the pool a few streets over. She didn't learn that town by the names of things. She learned it by heart through the practice of living.

That's what practices do—they bring an inner knowing deep down inside us. When we make time to pray, we enter into the mystery of knowing God. When we stop for a Sabbath, we learn that God is the creator and sustainer of all things. When we take time to renew our joy, we discover the gifts of God's good world. When we make time for friends, we remember where true riches in this life are found. When we work with a sense of mission and vocation, we embed the knowledge of our callings into each day. Good habits and practices help us learn and live by heart.

QUESTIONS TO ASK TO MEASURE YOUR PRACTICES

- What is a key practice you already do that shapes other smaller practices? For example, maybe making the bed every morning leads you to sort the laundry or stack your books.

- What practices have stood the test of time? A regular date night? A standing pickup game of basketball?

- How have practices helped you embed knowledge into your life? What are some things you don't even have to think about because you've done them so much?

- What spiritual practices have been most fruitful in your life with God?

■■■

EFFORT AND EARNING

At this point, you may feel your heart beginning to race or your stomach beginning to churn. Perhaps you're thinking, *My life is stressful enough, and this is starting to sound like a "Come on, do better!" kind of book. I don't need another inspirational challenge to live my best life or another list of steps to accomplish more.*

America is famous for its infatuation with efficiency and productivity. We don't know how to go slow or live small. We want to live large, to be bigger, better, and faster. Honestly, as a first-generation immigrant from Malaysia, I get the appeal of that obsession. I love America's propensity to dream big, to innovate and improve, to maximize *everything*.

But there are dangers in such a mindset. We can fool ourselves into thinking that success is growth, and our value as individuals is in our productivity.

This book, however, is not about increasing your productivity or improving your efficiency. It's not about self-help or slapping a Band-Aid on your hectic life. It's about something much deeper. Something that will shift you internally, transforming your entire posture and way of being so your life is sustainable and abundant—not just for you but for the Kingdom of God.

Intentionality is about abiding in Jesus—and allowing the Holy Spirit to produce his fruit in you for the sake of others.

Did you catch that? There are a few things in that statement worth unpacking. First, spiritual formation is the Spirit's work. The lead actor in this Big Story is the triune God—not you, not me. Intentionality creates space for us to sense the work of the Holy Spirit so that our participation is possible.

Second, fruitfulness is not the same thing as productivity. Productivity is about what we're *doing*; fruitfulness is about who we're *becoming*. That's why, when Paul listed the fruit of the Spirit in Galatians 5:22-23, he didn't mention achievements or accomplishments; he listed what might be called virtues: "love, joy, peace, patience, kindness, goodness, faithfulness, gentleness, and self-control."

Third, fruitfulness is always for the sake of others. An apple tree doesn't benefit from an apple . . . until the apple is eaten and the core is thrown on the ground, where the seeds can then turn into other apple trees (at least theoretically!).

We'll say it again: Growth happens on purpose, and cultivation requires intentionality. Good things flourish through attentiveness. Weeds grow on their own, but fruitfulness flows from faithfulness. Growing as a Christian means *abiding in Jesus and allowing the Holy Spirit to produce fruit in us for the sake of others.*

But, still, the question remains: Doesn't *becoming* involve some kind of *doing*? And whose work is it—ours or God's?

Maybe you're wondering, *Isn't all this talk of intentionality and purposeful growth just a new kind of legalism? Isn't it a form of earning our place with God through works?*

We understand the question. In fact, human beings are prone to keeping scoreboards of "enoughness" (a phrase from David Zahl's book *Seculosity*).[4] And when we find ourselves falling behind on the score, we develop systems of guilt management. So if the game is about reading the Bible more, the scoreboard is a Bible-reading plan or app. The app comes with its own version of guilt management, because if we fall behind in our reading plan, we know what to do to catch up. Or if the game is about our involvement in our children's lives, the scoreboard is the number of parties we plan or teams we volunteer to serve. And if we find ourselves losing—as we inevitably will—we can redeem ourselves by showing how often we read to our kids at night, or how well we prepare their school lunches.

The truth is, *anything* can become a game of winners and losers. We can turn even our best efforts into an attempt to prove our enoughness or atone for our "not-enoughness." But that's not the life in Christ God offers us. That is not the way of grace.

Yet God doesn't intend for us to do nothing about our growth. Sloth is not spiritual. As Dallas Willard wrote, "Grace is not opposed to *effort*, but [it] is opposed to *earning*."[5] The difference between legalism and spiritual discipline is not the work or energy involved; it's the motivation. Are we doing things to impress God and earn his favor? Or are we doing them because we are dearly loved children of God who are being conformed to the image of his Son by the power of the Spirit (Romans 8:1-17, 29)?

THE GIFT THAT GENERATES A RESPONSE

To get the motivation right, we have to rethink grace. The Greek word for grace is *charis*, which quite simply means "gift." In Western cultures today, we tend to think of grace as a gift with no strings attached. But in Eastern cultures and many cultures in the global south, a gift is meant to spark reciprocity. In Malaysia, when a neighbor brought our family a dish filled with food, my mum would never return the dish empty. She would send it back with something she had cooked. It wasn't a forced gesture based on pressure or obligation. It was a way of expressing gratitude and reinforcing the relationship. Gift giving in the West is linear. It moves from one person to the other and then ends. Gift giving in the East is circular. A gift can create or affirm a relationship; reciprocating the gift with another gift reinforces it.

During the Protestant Reformation in Europe in the 1500s, some preachers—in an effort to combat superstition, legalism, and the abuse of power in the medieval church—emphasized the notion of grace as a free gift. That was later modified—or distorted, as the case may be—by philosophers like Immanuel Kant, who thought of a gift with no strings attached as the purest ideal of a gift. But that's not quite how grace works. It's true that we cannot repay God for his grace. Nevertheless, grace is supposed to generate something in us.

Gratitude, yes, but also *obedience and allegiance to God, as well as service and generosity toward others.* The fear that grace somehow comes with hidden obligations has caused many Protestants to develop a kind of spiritual PTSD at the mere suggestion that God requires—and empowers!—his followers to work in response to his gift of grace. Yet the New Testament writers had no such aversion. Peter, no stranger to the slow, intentional work of becoming more like Jesus, challenged his congregation with these words:

> You must make every effort to add moral excellence
> to your faith; and to moral excellence, knowledge;
> and to knowledge, self-control; and to self-control,
> endurance; and to endurance, godliness; and to
> godliness, affection for others; and to affection
> for others, love. If all these are yours and they are
> growing in you, they'll keep you from becoming
> inactive and unfruitful in the knowledge of our
> Lord Jesus Christ. Whoever lacks these things is
> shortsighted and blind, forgetting that they were
> cleansed from their past sins.
>
> 2 PETER 1:5-9

"Faith without works is dead" (James 2:20, KJV). But none of our effort is effective without the Holy Spirit. A theology of works without a theology of the Spirit is legalism. For Paul and Peter and James and John, grace was found not only in the giving of Jesus Christ but also in the giving of the Holy

Spirit. Jesus did for us what we *could not do for ourselves.* The Spirit does in us and through us what we *cannot do by ourselves.*

Paul urged the Philippians to let salvation be embodied in their lives and practices, but he wouldn't let them forget that it was possible only because God was working in them:

> Therefore, my loved ones, just as you always obey me, not just when I am present but now even more while I am away, carry out your own salvation with fear and trembling. God is the one who enables you both to want and to actually live out his good purposes.
>
> PHILIPPIANS 2:12-13

Okay. That was a long stretch of theology. Let's pause for a moment and take a breath.

Everything we're about to share with you can be interpreted as doing more good works to earn favor with God. Please don't read it that way. Instead, hear this as an invitation to come to Jesus by the power of the Holy Spirit and participate in his work in your life so that you will bear fruit. All the practices we present in this book are *means of grace,* to use a more theological term from the English renewal preacher John Wesley. Spiritual practices don't earn grace; they help us receive it and take it deeply into our hearts and minds, bodies and souls.

Grace produces grateful generosity in us.

Grace fuels our fellowship with God.

Grace empowers our participation with the Holy Spirit's work in us.

In Christian tradition, spiritual practices are meant to be ways of abiding in Christ by the power of the Spirit so that we might bear fruit to the glory of the Father. Catch that. This is not a book full of new trends for proving our enoughness, attracting God's attention, or gaining his pleasure. We step into an intentional life as a *response* to his lavish love, fueled by his grace through the gift of the Spirit, to keep communing with Christ.

The providence of God doesn't cancel out our participation in his work. In Christ and by the Holy Spirit, we can now live out our original callings—our human vocations— to reflect the image of God and cultivate fruitfulness in the world for the sake of others. So let's be intentional about it. This year. Now.

The next two chapters involve the work of preparation, helping us look back and look forward prayerfully and purposefully. The five chapters that follow introduce a set of practices, or rhythms, that relate to five spheres of life— prayer, rest, renewal, relationships, and work. These practices enable us to pay attention to what's most important as we pause to reflect. In the final two chapters, we'll bring everything together, creating rhythms of intentionality and putting practices into action by enshrining them—if you will—on our calendars.

It works best if you read through the book slowly. Keep a journal at hand and stop every now and then to write down your ideas, including the practices you could adopt and the changes you'd need to make to integrate them into your life. Pray as you breathe in and out. Welcome the Holy Spirit and his work in your heart. You're reading not for information alone but to allow God to form your heart, soul, body, and mind for his work in you and in the world. So let this act of reading be done in an attitude of devotion.

Are you ready?

PART 1

REFLECTION
Looking Back and Looking Forward

We begin with preparation. Intentionality means we don't simply barrel ahead, making decisions and setting priorities blindly. We must first take inventory of our lives as they are: reflecting on the year that has passed or the season that is ending. Then, once we have a sense of where we've been, we can stop and listen to the Lord about the year or season ahead.

It would be easy to jump immediately to goals and plans and schedules and habits. But that would be a mistake. We are so prone to pushing onward that we fail to learn from the past. We miss the chance to mark the faithfulness of God in the season we've just come through. When we remember well—when we confess our failures and mark God's goodness—we put ourselves in the right posture to enter into the next season well.

This time of preparation echoes what the people of Israel did in the Old Testament before they entered the Promised Land. After crossing the Jordan River, they set up memorial stones to the Lord their God (see Joshua 4). They stopped to remember what he had done for them and who he had called them to be as his people.

There is a listening that precedes any doing, a waiting that comes before acting.

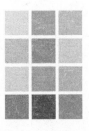

CHAPTER 2

REFLECTING ON THE PAST

Look at where you are.
Look at where you started.
The fact that you're alive is a miracle.
Just stay alive, that would be enough.

Eliza Hamilton, *Hamilton: An American Musical*

GLENN

We sometimes think intentionality is all about planning. It certainly involves that, but how can we plan if we don't stop and take stock first? When Holly is putting together a grocery list, she usually asks one of the kids to check the pantry and fridge to see what we're running low on. Contrast that with the times I just pop into the store and pick up a bunch of things we don't actually need!

Without taking inventory, we're all likely to make plans that simply add busyness and clutter to our lives. Remember, *activity is not the same thing as intentionality.*

So how do we take an inventory of our lives?

When the iPhone Screen Time setting was added a few years ago, it was a sobering way to check my own perception of how much time I spend on my phone and on various apps. I was convinced I picked up my phone mostly for work-related purposes, but alas, social media filled far too many hours. And speaking of "pickups," the number of times an hour I picked up my phone was deeply distressing. Before I started using Screen Time, if you had asked me how addicted I am to my phone, I would have said that I'm not. I would have told you I don't use it more than the average person, and I can totally set it aside for an hour. But the Screen Time report suggests otherwise.

Years ago when I began seeing a spiritual director, I talked to him about how I'd reflexively pick up my phone and refresh a few apps without even thinking about it. I'd pull down on the screen to refresh my Twitter time line and then do the same for Facebook and Instagram and my inbox. I told him I didn't like how twitchy I'd get, feeling the need to refresh these pages several times an hour. After listening and praying with me, he asked in a straightforward way what I might be doing to refresh *my soul* instead. Screen Time forced me to take an honest inventory of my phone use. But until that moment, I didn't realize I needed to take an inventory of my soul.

You may feel the same way about your life. You're coasting through just fine. You may be tired and stressed and busy, but overall you're sure you're doing okay. Until one day you aren't. The truth is, when we hit that wall, we find ourselves wishing we'd realized the true state of our inner world sooner.

Is there a tool that can help us assess the condition of our hearts and souls?

Indeed, there is. An ancient tool used in a new way.

Years ago, Holly and I discovered a practice that helps us discern God's presence in our lives. This ancient tool comes from Saint Ignatius of Loyola, who encouraged fellow believers over four hundred years ago to become aware of God in daily life.

Ignatius was a soldier who was wounded in battle. While he was recovering, he read a book on the saints that he had been given, and something awakened in him. Recognizing the vanity of his dreams of becoming a great soldier who was popular with the ladies, he surrendered his life to God. He lived with monks and paupers who were dying, and he spent extended time alone in caves to pray. When he emerged, he formed a community with friends who took vows of poverty and chastity.

They found a different way of *being* in the world. And they wanted to remain *in* the world. Ignatius and his companions—the Society of Jesus, or the Jesuits, as we know them—wanted to be contemplatives in action, finding God in all things.

Don't we all want to find God in everything? But most of us can't live as monastics. Holly and I have four children, whom we homeschool. We also have jobs and extended family and friendships and a community to serve. We can't just be absent from the activities of daily life. Yet there is a way to be present in them, to be intentional in the midst of living.

One of Ignatius's most helpful practices is known today as the Prayer of Examen. This practice is designed to help Christians prayerfully reflect on the events of each day and sense where the Lord is leading them. Many use this tool on a daily or weekly basis, which we highly encourage. But it can also be useful for reviewing a month or season. Holly and I have found it especially powerful for reflecting on an entire year. In fact, as Kyle Strobel and John Coe note in their book *Where Prayer Becomes Real*, when the Examen is used to review larger chunks of time rather than isolated moments of the day, major themes tend to emerge.[1]

Since this practice is most impactful when experienced, let's walk through it together.

THE PRAYER OF REFLECTION (EXAMEN)

Rest

HOLLY

Before you begin the Examen, sit in silence for three minutes. Slow down your breathing and welcome the Holy Spirit. Remind yourself that you are in the presence of the living God. The Holy Spirit lives in you and is working through you. He desires to have a living relationship with you.

If this is a new practice for you and you're struggling to focus your mind, you might want to visualize a peaceful place with Jesus sitting beside you. What would he be doing or saying to you? I often imagine sitting next to Jesus on a beach as we listen to the gentle roll of the waves on the shore and feel the sun shining on our faces.

Sometimes I also say breath prayers in my mind. A breath prayer is a prayer that can be spoken in one breath and repeated over and over. Many ancient Christians, including the Desert Fathers (monastic Christians in the third and fourth centuries), prayed the words *Lord, have mercy.* A longer form of this breath prayer is known as the Jesus Prayer: *Lord Jesus Christ, Son of God, have mercy on me, a sinner.* I often say, *Abba Father, I am yours.* Others pray breath prayers from Scripture, such as *When I am afraid, I will trust you* (paraphrase of Psalm 56:3) or *Not my will but yours* (Luke 22:42, NRSV), from Jesus' prayer in the garden of Gethsemane.

As you come to a place of stillness, let your heart find its center in Christ, the one who holds all things together (see Colossians 1:17). The Holy Spirit will guide the next few steps. Become aware of his presence and welcome his work.

Review

As you sit quietly, pay attention to how you're feeling before you begin a review of the year. How are you feeling physically? What emotions are you aware of? Are you feeling happy, sad, angry, anxious? Write down what you observe. I might write something like this in my journal: "8:30 a.m., stomach feeling unsettled, anxious about being away from the kids, joyful to see the snowcapped mountains out my hotel window."

Next, write down the significant things that happened over the past year. Reflect on your thought processes, your conversations, your actions. This might seem like a huge task, but write whatever comes to mind.

You might write down routines that flowed through most of your days or one-time events that impacted you greatly. Perhaps this was the year you became consistent in a workout routine. Maybe your grandmother passed in the summer, and you wake up every day thinking about how much you miss her. Or perhaps you became a single mom, and every day feels like a parenting crisis you have to carry on your own shoulders. One year I reflected on how often I talked with Glenn about my competing values of productivity and solitude and the way they consistently rubbed against each other. I wasn't getting enough space and quiet in my life, and it kept bubbling up in all my conversations.

When we review the days, weeks, and months of the previous year, we're giving God the opportunity to reveal to us what he's doing in our lives.

As you reflect on the past year, prayerfully ask God to bring things to mind. Ask him to show you where you've fallen short of his plan for your life. Ask him to make you aware of where or how you gave and received love or failed to do so. Ask, *What good could I have brought to someone but chose not to?*

A simple way to pray about this is to ask, *God, when have I said yes to participating with you this year, and when have I said no?*

Perhaps you sense the Lord leading you to read with your kids at night to connect with them, but you skip this part of the bedtime routine because you're tired. Could the Lord be prompting you to say yes to him? Or maybe when you stop at the local coffee shop on your way to work every morning, the same person wants to chat with you, and you try to dodge out quickly. Is the Lord asking you to say yes to loving this person, if only for a few minutes each day?

I'm often convicted by Jesus' words in Matthew 5: "Love your enemies and pray for those who harass you so that you will be acting as children of your Father who is in heaven" (verses 44-45). When the Lord asks me to love my enemies, my instinct is to shout, "NO!" Life is hard enough. Mustering up the ideas or the energy to show love to those who have hurt me or rejected me often feels impossible. And it *is* impossible without the leading and encouragement of the Holy Spirit.

QUESTIONS TO ASK AS YOU REVIEW THE YEAR

- What were some of the high points, or mountaintops, over the past year?

- What were some of the low moments, or valleys?

- What was an average day like? How did I feel in the morning and evening?

- What issues or problems, if any, did I struggle with this year? What recurring problems, tensions, or struggles did I experience?

- Where did I discover gifts of joy over the past year?

- Where did I experience sorrow and grief?

- Where or how did I give and receive love?

The year after I had our fourth child was one of the most difficult I've ever experienced. I had the typical feelings of a new parent: grateful we had a healthy baby, exhausted and weepy when I wasn't sleeping enough (which was often), overwhelmed and anxious about needing to care for four children. I had felt these things after giving birth to each of my other children, but this time, the overwhelmed and anxious feelings didn't seem to go away. As I sat in bed nursing my daughter Jane, who was a month old, I was highly aware of my other three kids running through the house. Anxiety took over. *How am I going to mother four children? I have too much to do. I can't possibly meet all their needs.* But somehow I kept going. I felt down but not bad enough to stay in bed. I felt anxious but not enough to keep me from engaging. Until it overcame me.

Four months into Jane's life, Glenn and I decided it might be good for me to leave town for a few days to breathe the fresh mountain air and maybe get some new perspective. It was October, one of my favorite months of the year. But this year it was difficult for me to see the beauty of the changing leaves or the vibrant, golden aspens around me. The mountain air and time with the family was good for my soul, but things quickly turned dark for me on the drive home. All along the interstate, signs were flashing an AMBER Alert. We soon discovered that a young girl in a nearby city had been kidnapped on her walk to school. For days we waited to hear of her fate. Part of me wanted to stop following the story, but I couldn't stop listening for updates. I hoped and prayed the story would end with celebrating her safe return. But I later learned that this little girl had been murdered not far from our home.

We hear these types of stories on the news more often than we want to. I've always been sensitive to the evil in our world, especially when this evil involves trauma for women and children. When I hear stories of violence against women, my stomach starts churning and feels like it's tied up in knots. When I hear of children who are abused, I'm deeply grieved, especially if their abusers were supposed to be their protectors. These events always affect me in some way, but this was different. Because of my constant postpartum anxiety, my normal ability to redirect my thoughts or choose to think about something else was impaired. I felt overcome with anxiety.

One evening I walked down the stairs and sat on a chair at our kitchen island. Within minutes I felt like I couldn't breathe. I was hyperventilating. I yelled to Glenn, "Something is wrong with me! I can't breathe. Am I dying? You need to take me to the hospital."

Thankfully, Glenn had walked with others through situations like this and knew what to do. He said calmly, "Holly, I think you're having a panic attack. Let's go outside and get some fresh air."

He helped me walk out our back door and then guided me through some deep breathing. Eventually I was able to calm down. Glenn brought me a cup of herbal tea and encouraged me to lie down for a while. After the panic attack passed, we realized that something needed to change. I wasn't getting enough sleep, water, healthy food, or help. I thought I could power through, pull myself up by my bootstraps, keep a smile on my face—but I couldn't. Most of our family was unavailable to help during this season, except Glenn's dad, David, who was living in Malaysia at the time. Words cannot express how grateful I am to him for coming to help us in a time of great need. He would sit with Jane and rock her so I could take care of myself for a few hours each day.

When I was reviewing this season several months later, I was aware of the depth of my own struggle and the gift of my in-laws being there for us. This season of difficulty was also a season of dependence on God and others. It was a profound experience of receiving love.

Rejoice

Rejoicing is an expression of gratitude that you can practice daily by verbalizing it to a spouse or friend or writing it in a gratefulness journal. It's also a wonderful practice to engage in as you review the past year. Reflect on the year month by month. What seemingly small things are you grateful for as you think about January, February, March, and so on? What are you grateful for that had a significant impact on you this year?

Write down anything that comes to mind. Thank God for the gift of his presence throughout the year, for blessings, for the gift of relationships, for the ability and opportunity to give and receive love. Maybe you're thinking of the blessing of a new-to-you car or the great insurance that comes with your job or a new baby added to your family. Or you might be thinking of how grateful you are for purple and pink phlox that bloomed yet another spring in your flower bed; or the warm, scrumptious tuna melt you enjoyed for lunch each day; or the daily view of the green, luscious rolling hills out your apartment window. Nothing is too small or insignificant to list here.

Writing down what we're grateful for helps us delight in and savor each of God's gifts. During our retreat last year, I struggled to remember all the things I had to be grateful for. As I sat in silence, asking the Lord to help me, memories of his goodness started coming to mind. The more I pondered his goodness, the more things I remembered. And my heart was filled with gratitude for all he had done. Like the psalmist, I wanted to say, "I will give thanks to you, LORD, with all my heart; I will tell of all your wonderful deeds" (Psalm 9:1, NIV).

I thought about how grateful I was to find a counselor who was a good fit—something I'd been praying about for a couple of years. As a trained counselor myself, I believe it's important to see a counselor during certain seasons of my life as I'm giving and pouring out to others through pastoral ministry and counseling. I want to practice what I preach.

I pondered how thankful I am for all my children, especially for this season with my older teenage daughters. I've felt excited for many years at the idea of having deep and thoughtful conversations with my kids, but I knew it would take time and patience on my part to wait for this season to come. Well, it's finally here, and I'm deeply grateful to God for all the ideas discussed at the dinner table and in the car or at the coffee shop. No topic is off the table. We've been talking about topics like politics, modesty, difficult Bible passages, dating, and social media, just to name a few.

At several points in this gratefulness exercise, I also named some of my closest friends and thanked the Lord for the privilege of spending time with them in prayer and meaningful conversation on a regular basis. Some I meet with weekly, and some once a month. However often we meet, I'm consistently grateful to the Lord to be known, strengthened, and encouraged by these wonderful women.

I also remembered that this year my lower back stopped aching every day. I'd injured it after about a year and a half of doing some intense workouts on a consistent basis. For many months, the constant pain had been a daily reminder that I couldn't control this piece of my life. I had to stop working out and ask the Lord to help me be content with walking and stretching. What a journey it's been. Delving into this gratitude exercise helped me remember where I once was and how far I had come.

Often in our full lives, we rush past all the ways God is showing his love or extending kindness to us. Once you've made your gratefulness list, engage in prayer with God. You could begin by saying, *Lord, thank you for blessing me this year and pouring out your love on me through . . .*

Repent

Next, we move from telling the Lord how grateful we are for all he has done in our lives to accepting where we have fallen short. Here, we repent and ask for forgiveness for the ways we did not cooperate with the Holy Spirit and failed to give and receive love. This is often the most difficult part of the prayer of reflection. It's definitely not a fun part for me, since I'm one to focus on what has gone well and where I've seen God working in his world. A friend of mine also finds this part of the prayer difficult, because she quickly moves to guilt and condemnation when focusing on where she has fallen short. If you resonate with this, ask the Lord to show you how to distinguish his voice of grace from your own voice of self-condemnation.

I'm reminded of the prayer of confession we pray every week in church: "We have not loved you with our whole heart; we have not loved our neighbors as ourselves. We are truly sorry and we humbly repent."[2]

As you enter this part of your reflection, ask yourself, *How have I not loved God with my whole heart this year?* Some years, I have written that I've failed to intentionally pursue my sister and parents in the ways I sensed the Lord leading me to. Years ago Glenn and I came up with the idea of going on a family trip with them every other summer. Being intentional about this gave all of us the assurance that even if we hadn't been physically together in months, we knew that that trip was coming and we would be together soon. One year I sensed the Lord leading me to intentionally "see" and empathize with one of my kids. I realized I had pulled away because it was difficult for me to connect with this child, but the Lord began to give me ideas of ways we could bond.

Glenn often repents of his lack of attentiveness to the family when he arrives home at the end of the day. His head and heart have a hard time transitioning from the swirl of conversations and decisions and tasks from his workday to kitchen chores, dinner prep, and time catching up with the kids. But when he reviews the year, he becomes aware of how little time we have left with them in the home. That awareness leads to repentance, turning away from the habit of frequently checking his phone and turning toward our children instead. It may even lead to a plan of leaving his phone in the car when he gets home!

Request

GLENN

As you end your prayer of reflection, ask the Lord for the grace to grow and participate with the Holy Spirit's work. Where do you sense the Holy Spirit leading you to grow this year? This might come easily to you, or it may take some time to rise to the surface. This past year, Holly sensed the Lord leading her into a year of greater wholeness and wellness. She felt there were areas in her life that she had neglected out of busyness or a sense that she needed to give most of her energy to our family or church family—all of whom she loves dearly. This nudge from the Lord motivated her to seek out therapy and a natural health practitioner to guide her on a journey toward being well, spirit, mind, and body.

Recently I sensed the Lord inviting me to relinquish control. In my desire to script the day or shape things by sharing insights, I can often be tightly wound and live with too much stress. I resolved not to be so scripted in my planning or share every observation or opinion with others. There were times to speak up and times to tell myself, *You don't need to have an opinion about that.*

In the fall of 2020, I developed a polyp on one of my vocal cords. I tried to heal it by resting my voice, not speaking for days at a time. I ended up having surgery and had to be totally silent for two full weeks—not even a cough or a laugh. For those two weeks, I had to limit myself to speaking for only five minutes every hour. Attending meetings was a great practice in making my words count. And it showed me I don't need to seize control and try to influence the course of a conversation. I can sit back and watch others lead and shine. Rather than being passive, I resolved to share power in healthy ways. As a result, I reduced my stress. I realized I had been overfunctioning, as counselors sometimes say.

I should warn you that asking God to grow you in a particular area can bring unexpected challenges. He might just grow you in ways you wouldn't choose. I'm not saying that God caused the problem with my vocal cords, but he did work through it to bring about the growth in my life that I had been praying for.

The best part of the gospel is that God always meets us with grace. Growth happens because of grace. Our request for growth, as it turns out, is really a request for grace.

REFLECTION AND RENEWAL

The goal of reflecting on the past year is to hold up our lives to God's light and present our whole selves to him. We often bring to God only the stuff that's going on right now, or the stuff we want to see happen. But the present and the future are only two-thirds of our lives. Inviting God into the past year—even the more distant past—is a way to find him in all things. We may have missed little signs of grace along the way, like little bread crumbs leading us home. We often fail to notice slight deviations in our habits or the calluses forming on our hearts. Usually by the time life forces us to notice, it's too late—like the driver who dozes off at the wheel and then jolts to attention when he finds himself drifting into oncoming traffic. The knee-jerk reaction that follows is often an overcorrection that has disastrous results. But safe and smart drivers handle changes on the road with small, frequent adjustments of the steering wheel. In a similar way, the Prayer of Examen, applied to the previous year, can help us present our lives before God, become aware of how he is working, and discover the intentional adjustments we can make to join him.

We encourage you not to hurry on to the next chapter. Take time to journal and write down your prayers and thoughts during each phase of reflection. This prayerful inventory taking is the necessary setup for what comes next. We cannot move into a new season without properly marking what has passed. Like ancient Israel setting up memorial stones at the Jordan River to commemorate what God did for them, provoking questions from their children that would allow them to tell the story again and again, so the practice of praying the Examen for a year or every six months marks a season and prepares us for the next one.

CHAPTER 3

A WORD FOR THE YEAR

There's a season for everything
and a time for every matter under the heavens.

Kohelet, Ecclesiastes 3:1

GLENN

When I was in college, I had the opportunity to travel with a rock band and play in arenas across the country. Well, that's how I heard the offer. It was really an opportunity to be the house band for worship leaders at some large youth venues. It was a boyhood dream come true.

I picked up the phone and punched in the international code and phone number of my parents in Malaysia. (Yes, this was the era of punch-button, plug-in-the-wall phones, before the internet had eliminated the need for these overpriced phone calls.) I sat at my desk in my dorm room, listening to the beeps, waiting for my dad to pick up.

My dad answered in his characteristically cheerful way, "Hi, Son!" He always seemed to know when I was calling. (Yes, this was also before caller ID.)

I told him that a worship leader who had just signed with a big record label had recruited us—little ol' measly college students in a worship band—to travel with him (or his guitar player, who also led worship) and lead thousands of young people in praising God.

"Wow!" my dad exclaimed. "How exciting!"

"But there's just one thing, Dad," I continued, this time without the upbeat energy in my voice. "I'd have to take a year off school."

Silence.

"But it's only one year. I'm working ahead anyway, and I'm on pace to finish early, so really this would just put me on a regular schedule."

Since my homeschooling high school years, I'd become famous for proposing alternate schedules and deadlines, accomplishing more some weeks than others. "Don't worry, Dad," I assured him. "I've got it all figured out." My dad still quotes these words back to me with a chuckle.

"Son," he replied slowly, with love and warmth in his voice, "I just don't think you should do it."

In the old days of international phone calls, every second

was precious. Calls from Tulsa, Oklahoma, to Malaysia were not cheap.

"Why?" was all I could muster in response.

Then came the words that have stuck with me for decades.

"Son, there will never be a shortage of good opportunities. But I think you have to ask yourself, 'What is this season for?' I think you came to America to go to college, not to be in a band."

He was right. I knew it. But I felt like this was my only shot to be in a band and travel and play in large arenas and lead thousands of young people in worship.

In the end, however, I realized this was not the season for traveling in a worship band. This was the season to submit myself to the process, to work hard in my preparation for life and a career, and to be faithful with the (home)work in front of me. What I couldn't have known then is that there was too much vanity in my desire to travel. My heart was drawn to the allure of influence. The process of purification will last a lifetime, but at twenty I definitely needed at least a few years of disciplined faithfulness before I could be trusted with a platform.

WHAT IS THIS SEASON FOR?

HOLLY

What is this season for? We should ask this question in every season of life. But how do we define a season?

The Bible uses two Greek words for time—*chronos* and *kairos*. The first has to do with chronological time, the sequential passing of days, weeks, months, and years. The second has to do with an appointed time, a special set-apart moment. If your birthday is in three months, the days, weeks, and months that pass until that event are *chronos* time. But the day of your birthday—which hopefully will include a celebration with friends and family—is a special moment, *kairos* time. So there are special moments or seasons that are set apart. But outside of these clearly set-apart times, how can we know when one season begins and another ends?

Seasons do not simply happen to us. When we choose an intentional life, we can also create rhythms that help us mark seasons. For example, many Christians mark time by using the church calendar, a way of marking seasons around the life of Christ. Marking a new season of life with the turn of a calendar year feels natural. I mean, that's when loads of people make resolutions. So there's not necessarily a spiritual reason to mark seasons by the earth's revolution around the sun. But since people around us mark time this way, and since we typically get a reprieve of a week or more from work and school, the waning days of a calendar year are a great time to take a retreat. Other opportunities to mark seasons may be at the beginning of a new school year or at the end of a busy season at work. Of course, you can easily set aside a couple of days for a retreat whenever you take vacation time.

The point is to know when you're going to set aside time to take an inventory of the past year. Don't leave it up to chance, and don't let it vary too much from year to year. Decide how you will mark the passing of one season to the next. Stop. Breathe. Reflect on the year gone by and then ask the Lord about the upcoming year: *What is this season for?*

Chronos, as the myth goes, was a man who gobbled up his children. If that isn't a parable about how time swallows our tomorrows, I don't know what is!

"Tomorrow, tomorrow," we keep saying, like Little Orphan Annie. We hope to have more time with our friends or make more memories with our children or pray more or get started on that house project . . . but tomorrow never comes. It gets gobbled up by the relentless march of chronological time. The time for action has passed; yesterday is gone.

The writer of Ecclesiastes mused about time and seasons:

There's a season for everything
and a time for every matter under the heavens:
a time for giving birth and a time for dying,
a time for planting and a time for uprooting what
was planted,
a time for killing and a time for healing,
a time for tearing down and a time for building up,
a time for crying and a time for laughing,
a time for mourning and a time for dancing,
a time for throwing stones and a time for gathering
stones,
a time for embracing and a time for avoiding
embraces,
a time for searching and a time for losing,
a time for keeping and a time for throwing away,

a time for tearing and a time for repairing,
a time for keeping silent and a time for speaking,
a time for loving and a time for hating,
a time for war and a time for peace.

ECCLESIASTES 3:1-8

Our toil must match the season. When I was a young girl, my dad would do different chores on the farm in different seasons. In the spring, it was planting. In the summer, it was mowing and baling hay. In the fall, it was harvesting. But even in winter, there were specific chores that had to be done, like feeding the cattle and providing warm bedding for them. Sometimes, when the weather wasn't too brutal, he would even walk around the farm fixing fences.

A wise farmer does the right work in the right season. A foolish farmer waits until he needs wood before chopping it. We don't want to wait until we're burning out before we stop. We don't want to hit a crossroads before we ask, "What is this season for?" There are pregame decisions we can make so that other decisions will be easier. There are proactive rhythms that can help us live with purpose and peace.

HEARING THE VOICE OF GOD

GLENN

I grew up in a church that believed in hearing the voice of God. I remember sitting in worship services in kids' church at an early age, listening for God to speak to me. What I heard in my heart wasn't earth-shattering stuff—just simple phrases like *I love you, I am with you, You are my child.* But for my eight-year-old self, it *was* earth-shattering. I needed to know those things.

Holly often felt pressure in church to hear God's voice, as if it were a booming sound from heaven. People around her seemed to hear God with such confidence and clarity. It left her feeling that because she struggled to hear his voice in a clear and emphatic way, there must be something wrong. Maybe she just wasn't good at it. Or maybe she was imagining things when she thought she heard a still, small voice whispering to her heart. It wasn't until her college years that she began to understand how God speaks to us. He works with our minds, feelings, and thoughts, not in some booming voice from heaven. (Though none of us would be opposed to that, either!)

It can be hard to parse out "what's me" and "what's God," but there are a few ways we can find assurance in discerning God's voice, especially as we listen for a word for the year.

Let's use this simple working definition: A *word for the year* is a theme, a phrase, a word, or even a picture that serves as a headline, or banner, over the next season. It should describe what God is doing and how we can join in. It's not a resolution or a goal. Those are focused on what we do. A word for the year is a word from God—a sense, a nudge, an awareness of what he is up to and how we can partner with him.

God will reveal himself to us in a variety of ways as we intentionally quiet our hearts and wait on him. We can learn to hear his voice by following a few simple principles.

Take the Posture of a Servant

The boy Samuel awoke to a voice calling his name. Dutifully, he made his way to the room where his master—Eli, the high priest in Israel—slept.

"Here I am!" Samuel called out.

The old man, eyesight dimming and hearing fading, fumbled around to see who was in his room. *Huh? What are you doing here?* he thought.

"Here I am," Samuel repeated. "You called me."

"No I didn't. Go back to bed," the old man mumbled.

The boy walked back to bed, confused.

Once again the voice came. Again Samuel went to Eli's room and announced himself: "Here I am. You called." And again Eli sent him back, sure the boy was dreaming or sleepwalking or something.

It happened again, a third time. But this time the old priest caught on. *Maybe the Lord is speaking to the boy*, he thought. He told Samuel to go back to bed, but this time he added, "If the voice calls you again, present yourself to the Lord as a servant standing at the ready."

So Samuel dutifully returned to his room and waited quietly.

The voice came again. Now Samuel knew what to do. He answered, "Speak. Your servant is listening" (1 Samuel 3:10).

There is so much that can be said about what it means to hear the voice of God. There are deep wells from which to draw. The contemplative and charismatic traditions of the Christian faith offer many practices that help. But the starting point for hearing from God is found in this story of Samuel's call in 1 Samuel 3. The Bible says that prior to this encounter, Samuel "didn't yet know the LORD" (verse 7). The beginning of his relationship with God was *learning to listen*. It required taking up a posture of readiness. Before he ever heard God's message, Samuel was prepared to obey. *Your servant is listening.* It may be that those who are unwilling to obey will never hear the command. Or, as the old saying goes, "when the student is ready, the teacher will appear." When our hearts are surrendered, the Lord will speak.

Start with What Scripture Has Already Revealed

Thankfully, we aren't starting from scratch. Christians believe in a speaking God. Just a few lines into reading the Creation story in the Bible, we discover that God *speaks*! The God of Scripture is a God of self-disclosure, a God who has chosen to reveal himself to his people. He is not a God who stands far off and waits for us to chase him. Our God pursues us! In fact, while other religions may be defined by humanity's search for God, the story of Scripture is of God's search for us.

So when you want to hear from God, begin with the Bible. Even when you're asking God to give you a general theme or direction, a word or phrase for a particular season, the Bible is how he speaks to you. Or to put it another way, if the Holy Spirit is a painter and your heart is the canvas on which he paints a vision for this season, the Bible is the palette of colors he uses. If you're well versed in Scripture, you're giving the Spirit more colors to paint with. In a way, hearing those simple phrases from God when I was a child makes sense, because they reflected the Bible verses I knew:

"God so loved the world" (John 3:16).

"I am with you always, to the end of the age" (Matthew 28:20, ESV).

"You are all God's children through faith in Christ Jesus" (Galatians 3:26).

"I have loved you with an everlasting love" (Jeremiah 31:3, ESV).

The older we grow, the more convinced Holly and I become that these foundational truths remain for a reason.

What does it look like to start with Scripture when listening for a word or theme for the year? Maybe you could pray through the fruit of the Spirit in Galatians 5. Does the Lord want this to be a year of joy? Or peace? Or faithfulness? Maybe this is a year for cultivating self-control or gentleness.

Another place to begin might be with instances in the New Testament where "the will of God" for you is explicitly mentioned. For example, 1 Thessalonians 5:18 says, "Give thanks in every situation because this is God's will for you in Christ Jesus." Maybe this is a year of gratitude for you. Earlier in that letter, Paul says, "God's will is that your lives are dedicated to him. This means that you stay away from sexual immorality and learn how to control your own body in a pure and respectable way" (4:3-4). Perhaps you could pray about consecrating yourself to the Lord in a more serious way this year, or focusing on purity in your thoughts and actions. Or maybe, as Peter wrote, this is a year to stay consistent, since it is "God's will that by doing good you will silence the ignorant talk of foolish people" (1 Peter 2:15).

Listen for the Clear and the Quiet

HOLLY

We can be tempted to think that God speaks one way or another, not in a variety of ways—that he speaks either clearly or quietly. We hear words and phrases, or we sense nudges and impressions. Yet the Bible contains examples of all these ways. Some people had dramatic visions, like Isaiah and Ezekiel; some, like Jacob, had dreams that came in the night. Some were actually caught up into the heavens and had an extended encounter with God, like John and perhaps even Paul. Others made judgment calls, like the members of the Jerusalem council who thought it "seemed good to the Holy Spirit and to [them]" to make the decisions they did (Acts 15:28, ESV).

And then there's Elijah, who encountered God in both dramatic and understated ways in a span of a few weeks. In response to Elijah's prayer, God sent fire from heaven in a showdown with the prophets of Baal, and afterward, Elijah heard God not in a "powerful wind" or an earthquake or a fire but in a "gentle whisper" (1 Kings 19:11-12, NIV).

The point is this: God speaks to us in different ways at different times. Don't be narrow in your expectations. Every time Glenn and I go on our annual retreat, he quickly receives his word for the year. I tend to be suspicious of the speed at which this happens, but he does process most things quickly. And to be fair, there have been times when he's heard a different word the next day. I take more time, listening quietly and waiting patiently for nudges and impressions from the Lord.

Pay Attention to Repeated Themes

GLENN

As we see in the Lord's calling of Samuel, God often uses repetition to speak to us. So Holly and I have learned to pay attention to repeating themes over a stretch of time. One year I felt the Lord asking me to move toward restoration, to be a person of peace and repair some burned bridges in relationships. During the first few weeks and months of that year, I reached out and reconnected with some people I might have hurt, seeking to restore relationships that had grown distant. Where it was appropriate, I apologized. Some were friends I had alienated by my zeal in discovering new ideas or practices. Others were people I had failed to be there for in difficult times. The desire to repair what could be repaired had been stirring in my heart for weeks, or maybe even months, leading up to our year-end retreat. When I sat to pray about the word for the year, it became clear that *restoration* was the banner over the season.

There was a year when Holly spent a lot of time focusing on strengthening her overall health and addressing some lingering issues. She was reading, listening to podcasts, consulting with conventional and functional medical professionals, and paying attention to her emotional health. It became obvious when she sat down to reflect on a word for the year that maybe all these health-focused activities were invitations from the Lord to take an intentional journey toward *wholeness* and *wellness*. Those became her words for the year.

Sometimes, listening to our lives brings repeated themes to the surface that we begin to notice. Like the burning bush that caught Moses' attention, causing him to stop and turn aside to find out why the bush hadn't been consumed (see Exodus 3), the consistent thematic notes in our lives call for our attention. When we stop and begin to listen more closely, we may discover an underlying root system or a common thread that helps us identify what God wants to do in our hearts in a particular season.

Test Your Word with Trusted Friends

Solitude is a good place to begin listening to God, but community is where words are tested. We have a strange capacity to delude ourselves. We may think we're hearing words from God when they're actually just the vain imaginings of our own egos. That's why Holly and I tend to be suspicious of prophetic words about people being world changers and history makers. Does God only act in epic ways? Or does he shape the lives of those whose ordinary faithfulness becomes significant only when we see the larger picture of his plan?

On my own, I'm prone to imagine a word for the year that has to do with achieving more or gaining more status.

But by the grace of God at work in others in my life—most of all Holly!—I'm able to tune out the noise of my own ambition and discern the leading of the Lord.

A trusted group of friends can help you not only discern your word for the year but also hold you to it. One year I was on a day retreat with a group of guys who have all been close friends for the better part of two decades. I shared with them my word for the year: *peace.* They listened and encouraged me as I shared about the frenetic pace of prior years, when there had been much activity and productivity, and how I sensed the Lord inviting me into a place of rest. Later that day I told them I was feeling a bit of pressure to get going on my next book but wasn't ready to put a proposal together. Frankly, my creative-output muscle was a little fatigued. But I didn't want to miss the window for publishing. That world can sometimes have unrealistic expectations about the rate of production. My friends—my dear brothers—listened and then echoed the words I had spoken that morning: that this year was to be a season of peace and rest. They reflected back to me the sense of weariness and angst they were hearing in my voice when I talked about writing again. The decision was clear: delay the writing process.

QUESTIONS TO ASK AS YOU LOOK AHEAD

- Have you ever sensed the voice of God? When has it been clear? When have you struggled to know?

- Think for a moment about the season you've just been through. Are there any themes or patterns you observe?

- What might be some of the lessons the Lord has been trying to teach you? What areas is God inviting you to grow in?

- Think of a time when friends and family helped you discern the voice of God. What lessons can you take away from that experience?

TRUSTING THE TIMING OF GOD

A word for the year is not a New Year's resolution. It's not a way of looking back and evaluating whether you accomplished or achieved something. Spiritual growth doesn't work that way. You never check the box on a fruit of the Spirit, as if to say, "Well, I've got *that* down. What's next?" What Holly and I have discovered, often the hard way, is that life tends to be about learning the same lessons at progressively deeper levels. We spin in orbit around Jesus in ever-widening circles, learning, for example, what patience looks like in this context or season. Spiritual growth is not linear; it is, in a sense, a spiral. Deeper and wider we go around a set of virtues defined by the center, Jesus himself.

So we never graduate from grace. We never outgrow our need for God—Father, Son, and Holy Spirit. That might seem discouraging, but it's actually good news. We weren't made to live independently from God. In fact, one way of understanding the original sin in Eden was that Adam and Eve wanted to be *like* God without being in communion *with* God. Like the moon reflecting the sun, we are radiant only when we reflect our glorious God. That's what being made in his image is about: We reflect God's wise and loving order and rule to the world so that what God created will flourish. But we don't accomplish this work apart from him. It is always God at work in his world *through* us.

In the book of Ecclesiastes, the Teacher wraps up his poetic discourse on the timing and seasons for all things by reminding listeners that it is God who has "made everything beautiful in its time" (3:11, ESV). God is the one who will do this. We don't listen for a word for the year so we can receive our marching orders and then carry them out on our own. We listen so we know how to walk in step with God as he works out his purposes in our lives and in the world. The Teacher goes on to say in the same verse that God "has also set eternity in the human heart; yet no one can fathom what God has done from beginning to end" (NIV). We long for our lives to echo into eternity, for our work to matter beyond the moment. Yet only God sees the whole picture.

That means there is freedom to confess our capacity. We can be honest about what we can and can't do. Be wary of words for the season that are always about "taking new ground" or "conquering a mountain" or "pressing on." Sometimes what we need is to pause, to slow down, to wait, to hold, to remain steady.

Every season has *limitations* and *invitations*. There are things God is asking us to say no to and things he is inviting us to say yes to. There are limitations we must accept and opportunities we must step out into. Like my story at the beginning of the chapter, I had to accept the limitations of being in college and embrace the invitation of that season of preparation. Discerning what a season is for involves recognizing the gifts and the griefs, the limits and the opportunities. That's why we step into this practice only after praying the Examen. As we grow in recognizing the grace of God at work in our lives and become more aware of his presence with us through the consolations and desolations that come, we can sense the way he is leading us. It won't be without messiness and mistakes, of course. But God honors our desire to listen and obey.

So stay close to the Lord. Listen and surrender. Abide, and you will bear fruit.

PART 2

INVENTORY
Examining Five Spheres of Life

Now that we have spent time preparing ourselves, we turn our focus to five specific spheres of life that deserve our attention and intentionality. Though in reality these spheres overlap and interlock, it's helpful to name them separately so we can take a more detailed inventory of our lives. Each sphere represents a value, something worth prizing and prioritizing on purpose.

As we look at each sphere of life—prayer, rest, renewal, relationships, and work—we'll pay attention to where God shows up, focusing on the biblical and theological foundation for each aspect of our lives. We'll also identify ways we might engage intentionally in each of these spheres by integrating specific practices, or rhythms, into our lives. All these practices can be embraced in every season of life. Where we anticipate objections due to the particular demands of marriage and children, we've tried to tell stories that might provoke your imagination for how this could look. But we certainly don't want to give the impression that certain practices are only for folks who are married with children! Again, this is for everyone. As you read, your own prayerful imagination will be required in seeing what each sphere might look like for you.

The chapters that follow will help you visualize the lay of the land—the spaces and ways your life unfolds. As you orient your focus to specific spheres and rhythms of your life, you allow your heart and mind to move toward freedom, peace, and purpose in each of these areas.

CHAPTER 4

PRACTICES OF PRAYER

*Prayer enlarges the heart until it is capable
of containing God's gift of himself.*

Mother Teresa

GLENN

I don't know when it happened. There wasn't one specific moment, or a catastrophic event. But I was becoming spiritually dead. I had never stopped to ask the question or slowed down enough to see the death spiral. When I read Henri Nouwen's words in *In the Name of Jesus* that for those in vocational ministry *burnout* is often a psychological term for "spiritual death," I realized that someone had just diagnosed my condition.[1]

Months earlier, the scandal involving the founding senior pastor of New Life Church, where I'm on staff, had made international news, and I moved from shock at his secret sin to soberness about the state of my own soul. I may not be able to pinpoint when I started dying inside, but I can tell you when I became aware of it. Reading Nouwen's book, I realized that this crisis was an invitation from the Holy Spirit to draw near to the Lord again. With repentance came a hunger to actively grow in intimacy with him. I realized that in ministry life it is all too easy to confuse busyness with fruitfulness, working for Jesus with abiding in Jesus. I was leading worship and mentoring people and teaching and preaching, but inside I was dying.

Serving Jesus is a crucial part of our life with God, but it is no substitute for actually renewing our relationship with him. When Jesus called his disciples to follow him, he called them to himself, to *be* with him before he sent them out.

As I leaned into the invitation to renew my relationship with the Lord in the waning months of 2006, I began a quest to learn about spiritual practices. Holly and I read various books and attended different worship services and events that introduced us to the spiritual practices that Christians had observed for thousands of years but were entirely new to us.

Maybe you have a full menu of spiritual practices that help you pray. Consider this a refresher course. Or maybe you feel stuck, like prayer is a tired and, quite honestly, boring practice. Great. We have some ideas for you. But our goal isn't to share fancy, new approaches or tricky techniques.

We want to introduce you to well-worn pathways of prayer. Some are new ways of saying old prayers. Others are just ancient practices that many of us have forgotten. Like treasures in Grandma's attic, these patterns of prayer in the storehouse of the church can inspire you. We want to share just a few of them with you. We've chosen less familiar practices of prayer in the hopes of spurring you on to a fresh journey as you pursue the intentional life. The four approaches we'll explore are psalm praying, the P-R-A-Y prayer, silence, and *lectio divina*.

PSALM PRAYING

We all know we *should* pray. In fact, I bet if we were to survey Christians about a spiritual practice that helps them grow closer to Jesus, prayer would rank number one, or near the top. I am equally sure that if we were to query how Christians feel about their prayer lives, they would say they need to pray more. (Don't we all.)

The problem with prayer is not usually motivation. We want to pray. It's just that we aren't always sure *how* to pray. Many people keep lists of people's names and the things they're going through. That's helpful, of course. There are also myriad prayer guides that walk us through various prayer points around the world or in our own country. All these are good. But while they tell us *what* to pray for, they still don't offer much help with *how* to pray. They might even operate on the assumption that we already know how to pray. After all, prayer is "just talking to God," right?

Well, yes and no. There are certainly no formal rules that govern how we should pray. Remember the story Jesus told about the man who beat his chest and said, "God, have mercy on me, a sinner" (Luke 18:13, NIV)? That kind of raw honesty is at the heart of prayer. But even in saying that, I'm implying that there are certain things to know about how to pray (e.g., being honest is good; being pretentious is not good). How do we discover those guiding principles without turning them into a set of rules to memorize?

The answer is right at our fingertips: We begin to pray with the people of God by praying the Psalms.

For roughly three thousand years, the Jewish people, from Bible times up to the present day, have used the Psalms as their prayer book. And for two thousand years, Christians have done the same. In fact, Christian leaders in the early centuries of the church believed that psalm praying was for everyone. In the early AD 400s, a pastor named Jerome said that farmers were to pray the Psalms while plowing their fields and workmen and shopkeepers should do so while going about their day. Eventually, psalm praying became a regular practice of those in spiritual communities who had taken vows. In the AD 500s, Saint Benedict had his monks pray through the entire book of Psalms in a week. Later, during the Protestant Reformation in Europe in the 1500s, the English archbishop Thomas Cranmer designed a pattern for Christians to pray through the Psalms together every month during morning and evening prayers. Martin Luther, the great German Reformer, said that when he felt "cool and joyless in prayer," he would take the book of Psalms and rush to his room to pray several of them.[2] No one is too high or too low in social standing, too mature or too new to the faith to gain by praying the Psalms.

I began praying through the Psalms a little over ten years ago. I do it almost daily, even if it's just one psalm. During the COVID-19 pandemic in 2020, our church invited the congregation to pray the Psalms daily together. We created a closed Facebook group, and every weekday morning at eight o'clock, someone would read aloud three or four psalms, stopping every few lines to add an extemporaneous prayer of agreement.

Praying extemporaneously alongside the Psalms is kind of like learning to paint by imitating great artists and then adding our own spin. Or like learning to play the piano as a child. We don't sit children down and say, "Just play what you'd like." That may get them comfortable with the instrument, but eventually they need to play someone else's compositions so they can internalize how composition works and then write their own music.

The first thing we discover when we pray the Psalms is that prayer is a *learned* language. Our native tongue is *selfishness*. Left to our own devices, we would pepper God with all our desires, needs, and demands. But praying the Psalms teaches us how to praise and petition and protest. The people of God have submitted to this school of prayer for thousands of years.

The second thing we discover when we pray the Psalms

is that prayer is a *personal* language. The psalmists weren't polished, prim, and proper pray-ers. They spoke in raw cries for help, laments over feeling abandoned, anguish over sin, jubilation for God's victory and deliverance, and praise for his unending faithfulness.

We cry out to God in our need like a baby crying out for her mother. The most eerie sound in a room full of babies is silence. In his book *Adopted for Life*, our friend Russell Moore recounts a heart-wrenching experience of visiting a Russian orphanage.[3] The silence he encountered was a silence of resignation to the fact that no one cared and no one was coming. If we believe that God cares for us and that he acts in space and time and history, we will keep crying out to him. When Jesus taught his disciples to pray, he told them to call God their *abba*, an intimate word for "father." The Psalms are filled with that sort of intimacy and immediacy with God. (Jesus reminds us here that we must all be taught to pray, and model prayers are one of the best ways to learn.)

Third, when we pray the Psalms, we discover that prayer is a *communal* language. Even the most personal psalms were written in a community prayer book. These were not secret journals. Think of Psalm 51, David's prayer of confession after his sin with Bathsheba. The last verses refer to the walls of Jerusalem being in ruins. The walls were not in ruins in David's day, but they were generations later when the Israelites were exiled to Babylon. The prayer of repentance King David prayed after his sin of adultery became a national prayer of repentance for the Israelites after their sin of spiritual adultery—idolatry.

Praying the Psalms helps us learn the deeply personal and communal language of prayer that renews us and places us in the story of God and his people. It's not hard to do. Simply open the book and read aloud one or two psalms a day, stopping to repeat a verse or spin out your own words based on that verse. Some verses—or entire psalms—may feel far too vengeful and difficult to pray. But as you begin to understand the circumstances and raw emotions the psalmists were experiencing, you will gain a deeper appreciation for these prayers. It might even make you honest about some of the darker emotions you've experienced but are unsure what to do with. The Psalms teach us to let every emotion be an occasion for intimacy with God. We can present our whole lives before God, not just the cleaned-up and sanitized bits.

Don't be afraid to start praying the Psalms. God often meets us not in isolated, epic moments of prayer but in the cumulative, long-term practice of prayer. To help you on your way, we've included a variety of excellent resources in the online appendix (glennpackiam.com/intentionalyear).

PRAY

HOLLY

Our God is not distant and distracted by other situations and people; he is relational and accessible at all times. Though we can pray to God anytime and anywhere, Glenn and I have found it helpful to include a consistent prayer time in our individual morning routines. Our friend Pete Greig has developed a simple acronym that has enriched our prayer times:

P—Pause
R—Rejoice
A—Ask
Y—Yield[4]

With these steps to guide me, I'm able to pray more consistently and thoughtfully. As I *pause* to be with God, I *rejoice* in what is good and *ask* him not only for what I need and desire but also for what others need. And ultimately I *yield* to his will.

Actually, this is a good guide to use anywhere! We can pray without ceasing by worshiping God with our everyday lives. If God is everywhere and in everything, then every act of love and kindness is a form of prayer.

When I had four kids seven years of age and under, I felt so overwhelmed that I could barely find a quiet moment to pray. In that season I felt the Lord leading me to view every act of service to my kids as an act of worshiping him. Every time I picked up my baby when she cried, every time I changed a diaper, every time I fixed a meal for the kids, every time I read a picture book, I was serving the Lord. We can offer God those moments more intentionally by simply pausing, rejoicing, asking, and yielding. Seriously. It can be done in about two minutes at various points throughout the day. Try it!

SILENCE

GLENN

With four children, two of whom are now teenagers, our house is almost never silent. The older I've gotten, the more introverted I've become. I long to spend a few moments alone in silence. I confess that when an appointment is canceled, I secretly rejoice. But here's the thing: I don't often make time to be alone. As an Enneagram Three with a Two-wing, I often see which chores need to be done in the kitchen or which child needs some one-on-one time, and I fill up what little margin we have in a thousand ways.

I began seeing a spiritual director in 2013. Somewhere between a counselor and a pastor, a spiritual director is trained to help you pay attention to what the Lord is saying and doing in your life. Spiritual directors don't usually have the technical training counselors have or all the theological training some pastors have, but they are brilliant listeners who can make connections and ask probing questions.

One of the things my spiritual director recommended was taking a two-day silent retreat. Because of my role as a pastor, he knew there were many demands on my time and attention and I was often tempted to ignore the condition of my soul. After he had suggested this for a few years, I finally decided to give it a try.

I reserved a room at a Jesuit retreat center about an hour's drive away from our home and arrived on a summer day in 2016. The grounds of the retreat center were beautiful, with walking paths, strategically placed benches and hammocks, and acres of well-tended grass. The center sat on a little hill, and the views evoked tranquility.

After setting my stuff down in my room, I took a stroll. I stopped and journaled, staring out at the beauty of creation. I popped in some earphones and listened to the book of Romans as I lay on a hammock. Then I walked some more and read some more.

I thought I had been there for days. Alas, only a few hours had passed. Just before dinnertime, I contemplated driving into the closest town to eat at a restaurant and hear human voices.

As I sat in my car, I decided to call Holly. "Babe, I can't do this," I told her.

She laughed and then encouraged me to keep going. Somehow I made it to morning, which, mercifully, was a Sunday. The chapel at the retreat center doubled as a church, so I joined the service, never more grateful to hear the low rumble of conversations in the pews.

In today's hyperconnected world, we aren't often silent or alone. Yet it's in those quiet moments we become present to the Lord and the Lord becomes present to us.

The year 2020 brought "unprecedented" (I just had to use the most overused word of that year) disruption to people all around the world. I was no exception. As I shared earlier, in the fall of that year, I developed a polyp on one of my vocal cords. In spite of resting my voice as much as possible, I still sounded hoarse. A month or so went by before I finally decided to see a local ear, nose, and throat doctor.

He discovered the polyp right away and recommended surgery. I was hesitant, wanting to see if time and various therapies could heal it. More than a month later, after seeing a specialist in Denver, I realized that there was no getting around reality: I needed surgery to have the polyp removed and a bleeding vessel ablated. Holly and I ended up flying to Boston, where some of the leading vocal surgeons in the world performed the surgery (thank God for insurance!), and by God's graciousness, it was a success.

But between the vocal rest I submitted to in an attempt to preempt surgery and the vocal rest mandated after the surgery, I spent about thirty days in total silence over a span of about two and a half months. I became so good at silence, I felt like a monk. (Friends and family members who knew my struggle at the silent retreat didn't fail to point out the major irony of this.) Of course, there were also several comedic moments when I tried to act out my words charade-style, which was especially hilarious when parenting our younger kids!

This season of silence allowed me to be present to myself and to the Lord in a powerful way. I began to realize that many of the times I wanted to speak were out of frustration or even anger. I wanted a child to quit fighting with a sibling, or my teenagers to clean up after themselves in the kitchen. I also realized how often fear rises to the surface in my heart. Both anger and fear are related to the desire for control. I became attentive to that and began to pray about how to deal with this impulse. As I journaled and prayed, I recognized only two healthy kinds of control. One type of control is what social scientists call *agency*—the sense of being able to direct your life according to your values and convictions. The other is spurred by care and concern, though perhaps *control* is too strong a word. Because, in the end, control is an illusion.

We are not in control, but we are deeply loved by the God who is.

The silence also led me to reflect on the ways God is in control. My thoughts crystallized around a notion of control that was less like a puppet master pulling all the right strings and more like an attentive, presiding presence. Actually, a very close presence who suffers alongside us and saves us sometimes from our situations, and at other times *through* them.

Silence can be embraced as a pathway of renewal. In today's world of tweets and likes and going live on social media, we desperately need digital silence. Instead of constantly refreshing our phone apps, we need to prioritize refreshing our souls.

LECTIO DIVINA

HOLLY

Lectio divina is a form of sacred listening that involves reading a passage from Scripture and meditating on it for a few minutes; then rereading it often, meditating on it again, and soaking in it. The idea is to imagine yourself on the scene in the story you're reading or to ask God to help you notice particular words or phrases in a psalm, letter, or passage. What do you see, sense, feel in the moment? When we read Scripture this way, we give the Holy Spirit the opportunity to make Scripture come alive in our hearts rather than merely fill our heads with information. Rather than trying to interpret Scripture for ourselves, we allow the truth of Scripture to permeate our lives.

Eugene Peterson said it this way:

> *Lectio divina* is not a methodical technique for reading the Bible. It is a cultivated, developed habit of *living* the text in Jesus' name. This is the way, the *only* way, that the Holy Scriptures become formative in the Christian church and become salt and leaven in the world.[5]

If you're looking for a guided experience, Lectio 365 is a great app that Glenn and I have used to contemplate the Scriptures and pray. With calm instrumental music playing in the background, the narrator—who changes from week to week—invites you to pause, listen to a Scripture passage, reflect on what you notice and what God might be saying, listen to the text again, and then offer God a prayer of response. The entire exercise takes about seven minutes and is a wonderful way to begin or end the day with God's Word.

Years ago I met with a wise, seasoned, and faith-filled believer, Phyllis, whom I asked to mentor me. I was a twenty-something pastor's wife who knew little about the vocation or the depth of God's Word. I desperately wanted to understand the Word of God and discover how precious it was. One of the Scriptures we meditated on stuck with me: "Your word is so pleasing to my taste buds—it's sweeter than honey in my mouth!" (Psalm 119:103). The practice of *lectio divina* invited me to allow God's Word to dwell deeply in my heart. I pray it will help God's Word come alive in your soul.

A PLETHORA OF PRACTICES

Our goal in sharing some of our favorite prayer practices is simply to get the ball rolling for you. You'll have to find the practices that fill in the gaps of your own formation. Since we don't always see ourselves fully, some trusted friends and family members can often help us discern these gaps.

If you've been following Jesus for a while, you may notice that certain practices can become stale; it can feel as if you're just going through the motions. We want to say two things about that. First, there's nothing wrong with consistency and habit. Rituals can be empty, robotic practices, or they can be powerful ways to reinforce our good desires. (For example, we desire clean, healthy teeth, so we embrace the ritual of brushing our teeth even when we don't "feel" like it!) Just as physical rituals develop good muscle memory, prayer practices develop good spiritual memory that leads to growth. You may not see results in the short term, but stick with it and see what happens down the road.

Like rituals, ruts can be good or bad. They may be well-worn trails that keep us moving in the right direction, or they may be muddy tracks that get us stuck. To avoid the latter, we need to revisit and refresh the prayer practices we're engaging in.

Second, it's good to diversify your portfolio of prayer practices. Spiritual practices are like an investment choice, and as every financial adviser knows, diversity is key. One prayer practice may produce more growth than another, and it can be good to have an array of practices to choose from.

For those of us who serve actively in a local church, we sometimes need to seek out practices that are different from those we're used to. For example, Holly and I love modern worship; the energy and vibrancy move us deeply. And yet because we participate in so many worship services like that, we often find a choral evensong renewing, or we enjoy listening to a Scripture meditation app. Being introduced to ancient prayer practices has also brought freshness to our lives with God. The switch-up awakens our brains and gets our neurons firing in new ways.

It may be tempting to add five new prayer practices to your life to create some freshness and excitement. But we encourage you to start small and focus on practices that are sustainable. An important part of intentionality is sustainability. Being consistent with two or three practices is far better than trying to keep four or five practices going but dropping them in the end like a juggler with too many oranges in the air.

The intentional life begins and ends with the Father, Son, and Holy Spirit, who sustain all things. Prayer isn't simply one sphere of life, or one category or compartment. It is foundational to life. But it takes many forms. And sometimes the forms that function well in one season fail us in the next. Some of us are wired for change, and a new practice brings fresh perspective. Others love consistency and feel more of a need to tweak rather than overhaul their prayer practices. Wherever you find yourself on this continuum, pay attention to what God is up to in your life—and keep revisiting and refreshing your practices of prayer.

QUESTIONS ON PRACTICING PRAYER

- Jot down the way you pray. Is it spontaneous or scheduled? Do you sit and listen or walk and talk? What practice of prayer do you default to?

- Prayer often resembles human connection. Consider what helps you connect with other people. Is it more cognitive or emotional? What makes you feel loved? Which prayer practice most resembles that type of connection?

- Think about getting up tomorrow morning to engage in prayer in your default mode. Do you dread it or look forward to it? Sometimes discipline and diligence are the answer; other times, provoking delight is necessary.

- Which of the prayer practices we explored in this chapter is new to you? Consider testing it out for a short time. Take a few weeks and only pray in that way. See what effect it has on your life with God.

- Choose one or two prayer practices and keep a simple log of your observations as you engage in each practice. Paying attention to how you pray today will help you be more intentional about prayer tomorrow.

CHAPTER 5

THE POWER OF REST

Most of the things we need . . . to be most fully alive
never come from [busyness]. They grow in rest.

Mark Buchanan, *The Holy Wild*

HOLLY

We lit a tiny, very-average-looking candle at the start of Sabbath on a Friday afternoon. Staring into the amber light, I was flooded with memories of our Sabbath practices from years past. When Glenn and I first started learning about the spiritual practice of a weekly Sabbath about eleven years ago, we became quite zealous and intentional about it, determined to make it part of our family life. In that season, we lit a "special" candle each week, dropped all our screen devices in a basket, and said a prayer to guide us into the next twenty-four hours.

Sabbath was a dedicated time we purposely set aside each week to stop and rest from regular work activity and delight in the Lord and his people. Over the years, though, we've struggled to be consistent in practicing a Sabbath rhythm. Or it might be better to say we practice a kind of messy Sabbath. Many times, just as we thought we were getting into a regular, healthy routine, something like an extended sickness or a new soccer season—or the birth of another child—would derail our rhythm. So we would pause to reevalute, asking ourselves, "When during the week do we have the best chance of setting aside twenty-four hours for Sabbath?" We've found that it changes in various seasons year to year.

In this current season of our lives, with our kids ranging in age from ten to seventeen, it's quite challenging to consistently practice Sabbath. Our older girls are involved in a theater company four months of the year, and our son is in competitive soccer nine months of the year. We've decided that Saturday is still the best day for a family Sabbath, and we keep it with the kids who are home. A typical Sabbath in this season begins with Glenn and me sneaking out of the house early in the morning for a date at a local coffee shop down the road. We get back midmorning as the kids are just getting up for the day, and we all enjoy a leisurely breakfast of eggs, pancakes, bacon, toast, and coffee. Then we create space for family devotions. Sometimes, we'll worship together and watch a BibleProject video on a book of the Bible. The middle part of the day usually involves each of us spending alone time or time with God, and then we'll all do something together, like hiking or playing a game. As evening approaches, we'll gather for dinner and a time of reflecting on the day or week. And then we might end the day with a family movie.

Sabbath in its simplest form is about stopping. But in our crazy, frenetic, interconnected, always-on world, stopping takes some preparation. You can't just ignore your emails (though I am tempted to!); you have to set up an out-of-office message. You can't just avoid the kitchen; you have to think about what you'll eat. So let's look at Sabbath in two parts: the external preparations and the internal posture of rest.

PREPARING TO REST

For me, truly being able to rest—as much as is possible with four kids—means preparing well. And preparing well means doing quite a bit of work around the home ahead of time. At times it seems counterintuitive to work, work, work—sometimes in a frenzy—to finally be able to rest and delight in the Lord. But I truly believe that if I put in a little more planning and work on the front end, Sabbath can be restful and filled with delight.

Our preparation for Sabbath looks like scurrying around a cluttered house picking up books, clothes, papers, and random bits of food that somehow traveled from the kitchen to other parts of the house. (We have a rule about eating only in the kitchen and dining areas, but my children, who don't always listen, have been known to walk around the house humming while eating crackers and dropping crumbs along their path.)

Anyway . . . our older teenage girls are extremely helpful in getting our home picked up and organized. One daughter in particular thrives in an orderly environment, so she is just as much an advocate of keeping things neat and tidy as we are. (I have to admit here that I'm more inclined to strive for tidiness prior to Sabbath than on most other days. I could spend all my time doing dishes, cooking meals, and picking up, and that doesn't feel like a flourishing life to me. Relationship rules the roost for us, and that usually means a somewhat untidy house.)

As we get ready for the Sabbath, we put the house back in order, get necessary groceries for the weekend, and prepare food. Unfortunately, as Glenn can attest, I struggle with having to think ahead about meal planning. If only I could point a wand and have a healthy meal appear! I'm determined to cook healthy meals, but it means spending endless hours making dressings and condiments from scratch, chopping vegetables until my hand hurts, and, well, not eating any sugar. Since our family continues to navigate some food sensitivities and health issues, food preparation requires that much more time and energy.

So it isn't restful or Sabbathesque for me to think about food. But thankfully, Glenn enjoys cooking! His creativity comes out in the kitchen. He throws a little of this and a little of that into a bubbling pot on the stove and usually comes up with some kind of culinary masterpiece. And for this I'm grateful. Our Sabbath meals are typically quite nice, since Glenn finds it restful to experiment in the kitchen.

Maybe you're in a phase where you wonder if taking a Sabbath could actually feel restful. I remember the days of having three kids five years of age and under and feeling as though the weight of Sabbath preparation was entirely on my shoulders. I recently talked with a friend who is a new mom. She mentioned feeling that taking a twenty-four-hour Sabbath, as the Bible suggests, was almost impossible considering all the factors and stresses of life involved in their current situation. But she could take two hours on a weekend day to find some silence, rest, and reflection—if her baby napped.

"Can you start small?" she asked me.

"Of course!" I assured her. And you don't have to do it perfectly from the beginning. Or ever, really. Perfection isn't the point. Abiding in Christ, not performing for Christ, is the goal.

I believe the Lord will honor the time we set aside to rest and delight in him, even if it's not an entire day. He asks us to take a Sabbath not only to attend to our relationship with him but also to give our whole being—body, mind, and spirit—time to rest.

We'll have nothing to pour out to others if we aren't first giving ourselves the gift of Sabbath rest. So what would you need to do to prepare for a Sabbath rest? What details do you need to take care of ahead of time? Clean? Grocery-shop? Plan meals and prepare food? Set up your out-of-office message? How could you manage the expectations of others on the Sabbath? Preparation for the Sabbath is a must, because rest only happens on purpose.

STARTING TO STOP

Sabbath rest can look quite different for each of us. When we consider what we want to include in a Sabbath day, we also consider things we need to cease from. For me, a perfect Sabbath would include elements of solitude, reading and reflection, nature, and play with our family. It would mean ceasing from the regular work I do during the week, such as housework, most cooking, my kids' education, and pastoral ministry. I frequently see or think of things that need to be done, and it's tempting to work on them rather than stopping for rest. Instead, I've learned to enter them in my to-do-list app to get them out of my brain so I can fully settle into a Sabbath rest.

But many weeks I feel like I can't possibly get everything done that needs to be accomplished in six days. I'm tempted to believe that things will go better for the family if I work nonstop. If I just keep working, and pushing, I'll get more done and eventually feel more peaceful.

But research has shown that this isn't true. In fact, several studies demonstrate that "people get more done when they work fewer hours, and less done when they work more hours."[1] I've found that I feel more rested and have more energy to start the week when I Sabbath well. In seasons when I work day after day with no breaks, I begin to wear down emotionally and physically and eventually crash. My body fatigues, and I become short-tempered with everyone around me. The goal of life shouldn't be to operate like a machine that produces nonstop. Living a fully human life means stopping and recognizing that the world will go on even when we stop contributing.

We often hear messages from our culture that tell us we need to focus on getting more and doing more. I'm constantly asking the Lord to remind me to be content and grateful whether I have plenty or little (see Philippians 4:12). But I'm still tempted to work more to find a sense of worthiness in my doing. The irony is that we can even try to get "more" out of a Sabbath—more rest, more reading, more renewal—and undermine the spirit of the Sabbath in the process!

Sabbath is not something to achieve. Sabbath is when I remind myself of who God is and who I am as his beloved child.

Lynne Baab observes,

The meaning of the word "sabbath" is "stop, cease, desist, pause, rest." The first question we need to address when beginning a sabbath pattern is, "What will I cease from?" Only after we have clarified that question can we move on to the second question, "What will I do on the sabbath to nurture my ability to rest in God?"[2]

There's nothing I can do to make God love me more. He won't love me more if I multitask or fill my schedule to the brim. When people ask, "How are you?" why do we say, "I'm so busy"? Is it because we feel good about ourselves or think we're winning God's approval when we can say we're busy and productive? I've started saying, "Life is full, but I'm trying to be present and enjoy each moment."

I've also been trying to internalize Ken Shigematsu's wise words:

> We need to ask ourselves *why* we are so busy. Sabbath helps us to question our assumptions.
>
> The truth is that we may be busy because we feel a need to validate our worth. Sabbath gives us a chance to step off the hamster wheel and listen to the voice that tells us we are beloved by God. The Sabbath heals us from our compulsion to measure ourselves by what we accomplish, who we know, and the influence we have. Sabbath enables us to define ourselves less by our achievements and more as beloved daughters and sons of God. As we become more aware of how much we are cherished as children of God, we grow in our trust of God.[3]

Sabbath is a chance to stop and listen to the wind blowing through the trees and my sweet child narrating a story. On one memorable Sabbath day, Jane and I spent some time playing games like Memory and Old Maid. It was a delight to hear her giggles as she schemed to get me stuck with the old maid.

Some holy moments are waiting for us if we'll only pay attention. I think about the early days of the COVID-19 pandemic—a devastating crisis that impacted not just our family and our neighbors but people in countries across the globe. It was heartbreaking to hear the stories of those who fell ill and were hospitalized, and even worse to learn of those who lost their lives. As government officials issued stay-at-home orders, I asked the Lord, *What do you have for me in this season?* In a way, it was like a forced Sabbath. I deleted all the events from my phone calendar—planned gatherings in our home, meetings, appointments, kids' activities, and outings with friends. Glenn and I suddenly had newfound space to reimagine our daily rhythms. What would we do with the time we'd been given? We had opportunities every day at home to have mini-Sabbaths. We took walks together almost every day and spent late afternoons preparing dinner together. My goal of reading aloud to my kids until they leave home had been a challenge as my fifteen- and thirteen-year-olds became more involved in activities. But this unexpected Sabbath-like season created space every night for me to read Lois Lowry's book *The Giver* aloud to them. What a gift!

The extended time at home during various moments of the COVID-19 pandemic also gave me space to ask, *What pieces of life that have been removed should be placed back onto our calendar? What parts of life are we called to continue in, and what things do we need to let go of?*

Sabbath keeping is certainly about setting aside one day of the week to rest, but it can also lead us to think about Sabbath seasons, times when we deliberately do less. The summer is like that for our family. But Lent—that six-week lead-up to Easter—is another opportunity to "fast," giving up something to make space for God. Stopping makes his presence possible. In that sense, certain seasons can be Sabbath-like. Consider that as you continue thinking about your year.

YOUR SABBATH

As you process how to plan a Sabbath day, take different factors into consideration. Are you single, married, or married with kids? Will you Sabbath alone or with others? Consider your personality. Are you introverted or extroverted? Do you work alone all week and crave time with people? Are you home with kids all week and needing some time alone with God? Or are you around people in an office all week and desiring some alone time on the Sabbath?

QUESTIONS TO ASK ABOUT SABBATH PLANNING

- When will I set aside a day for Sabbath?
- What will I do?
- What will I cease from doing?

POSSIBLE SABBATH ACTIVITIES

- Light some candles.
- Take time to worship.
- Take a walk and enjoy being in nature.
- Leisurely make and savor a meal.
- Play some games.
- Gather with family or friends.

QUESTIONS TO HELP YOU DECIDE WHICH ACTIVITIES ARE ACCEPTABLE ON THE SABBATH

- What activities are life-giving to you?
- What helps you connect with the Lord?
- What brings you rest?
- What brings you delight?

ACTIVITIES TO CEASE FROM ON THE SABBATH

- technology
- projects on your to-do list
- housework, chores
- shopping

LIVING FREE

GLENN

I'll be honest. I used to feel guilty for lying on the couch. As a chronic overachiever, I'm always aware of what needs to be done—dishes to clean, stuff to pick up, emails to reply to. Even my reading can be shaped by have-tos, not get-tos. *I need to finish another chapter*, I tell myself as I pick up a book.

But that's changing as I embrace the biblical vision of rest. God has pointed us toward regular rest from the beginning. Rest is not selfish or lazy but rather an invitation to abide.

In the Old Testament, the people of God were instructed to keep the Sabbath. These instructions are most clearly expressed on two separate occasions: at the giving of the Ten Commandments in Exodus and at the renewal of the covenant in Deuteronomy. Each time the command was given, a rationale accompanied it—something that happens only with a few commandments.

But the reason for Sabbath keeping is different in each instance. In Exodus, Sabbath is rooted in the Creation story: The Israelites were told to keep the Sabbath holy because "in six days the LORD made heaven and earth, the sea, and all that is in them, but rested the seventh day" (Exodus 20:11, NRSV). In Deuteronomy, the people of God were told to keep the Sabbath as a way of remembering God's deliverance: "Remember that you were slaves in Egypt and that the LORD your God brought you out of there with a mighty hand and an outstretched arm" (Deuteronomy 5:15, NIV). Sabbath keeping is grounded in salvation.

Something about the Sabbath reminds us of the two significant events in the Great Story: the creation of the universe and the salvation of humankind. Exodus and Deuteronomy together show us why we keep the Sabbath. We keep it to remember that God is the creator and sustainer of all things. In him—not by us!—"all things are held together" (Colossians 1:17). We also keep the Sabbath to remember that God has freed us and saved us. There are no taskmasters driving us, other than our own internal voices telling us we need to produce and achieve more.

Or to sum up the Old Testament rationale for Sabbath keeping in a slightly different way: *We rest because God rested, and we rest because we are free.*

When you pick up a book like this and look at the title, you might think it's about efficiency and effectiveness. As if being intentional is all about productivity. Well, it's not. Remember the difference we discussed early on between productivity and fruitfulness? That image of fruitfulness helps us recall a lesson from nature: If you overfarm a patch of land, you strip it of nutrients. If you want the land to be fruitful, you have to let it rest. God told ancient Israel that. And God tells us the same thing.

How are you creating room for rest in your life? Do you know when to stop, or do you tend to just go and go and go until you crash (get sick or exhausted)?

How do you feel when you sit around and are unproductive? Consider the difference between a Sabbath day and a day off. Sabbath is about returning to trust in God as the creator and sustainer. It's a way of reminding ourselves that he has delivered us from bondage. Yes, play and recreation are part of Sabbath, as we'll see in the next chapter when we explore pathways of renewal. But we cannot experience renewal without stopping first.

So when is your Sabbath? Make a plan. Choose a day or even half a day. Prepare for the Sabbath. Then stop. Really, truly stop. Be free.

CHAPTER 6

PATHWAYS OF RENEWAL

I rest in the grace of the world, and am free.

Wendell Berry, "The Peace of Wild Things"

GLENN

Vacations are great! But if you have kids, you know that your vacations are for memories, not for rest or renewal. Some years ago, when I got my first short sabbatical at the church, I thought it was going to be the most restful thing ever. And then I realized that I'm not a monk, and I don't live in a monastery. But I quickly learned that even during summer lulls or family trips I can build in practices to make sure I'm not just taking a break but am actually being renewed.

Look, sometimes we find ourselves stuck. Everything feels a little blah. The humdrum of life is more monotonous and uninspiring than before. We haven't thought about a new idea or taken a new risk or felt excited to get out of bed in the morning in a long time. There are many reasons for this, of course, and some of them are the result of serious, deeper problems. But for many of us, it's because we haven't taken the time for life-giving practices. There are ways that our minds and hearts are renewed, our bodies are refreshed, and our spirits are restored. We've discussed the spiritual practice of prayer in its various forms. We've explored the power of stopping to rest. But there are also practical pathways to bring life to our being.

There are many pathways of renewal, and we suspect they're going to be different for different personalities. We're all wired in unique ways. But in this chapter we'll describe a few practices that have been so life-giving for Holly and me that we have integrated them into our daily lives.

As you read about these pathways of renewal, think about practices you've already incorporated into your life. Consider what's missing. Reflect on how or when you could embrace other practices of renewal as you move into your next year or season.

RENEWING BODY AND SOUL

HOLLY

Renewing our bodies and our minds is critical for flourishing lives. For some of us, caring for these aspects of our lives might seem like work we don't have time or energy for. Or maybe we genuinely enjoy it but feel guilty about the time we spend on it. But taking care of our bodies and our minds is more than just an activity; it's as spiritual as prayer or worship. Listening to our bodies can be an important way to listen to God. What might he be trying to communicate to you through your body? Is he saying that it's a season to get moving or a season to engage more fully in rest? Have you been pushing your mind and body too hard, to the point of fatigue? As you think about spaces for renewal in your life, here are some important areas to consider.

Nutrition and Exercise

I've needed to put a great deal of time into researching health and food, as well as consulting with conventional and functional doctors, to figure out the best ways for me to stay healthy. As I've come to understand what I need in terms of food preparation, health advice, and exercise, I've learned that caring for my body and mind takes up a good portion of my week. I've felt the Lord prompting me to give attention to this area. Left to myself, I would much rather focus on other things.

Basic practices like walking outside every day, drinking plenty of water, and getting eight hours of sleep each night are essential for our mental and physical health. For years I'd been a night owl, but in the past couple of years, I've recognized that staying up late isn't serving me well. Now I go to bed earlier (around the same time every night) and get up early (around the same time every morning). Our body systems are all interconnected. The physical activities we engage in and the fuel we put into our bodies have an impact on us physically, mentally, emotionally, and even spiritually. I've found that when I get better and more consistent sleep, for instance, the rest of life is easier.

For those of you with babies or little ones who are greatly dependent on you, you might be getting a little stressed at this point. Even simple activities like exercising every day can be a challenge in your season of life. I get it. In the season when I had lots of little ones to care for, I thought I was doing well if I drank plenty of water every day, ate a relatively healthy meal here and there (whatever I could manage to prepare with kids all around me), and exercised a couple of times a week. And there were plenty of weeks during that season when I failed to accomplish even these basic tasks. (I was overwhelmed most days!) The key to intentional renewal through nutrition and exercise is to find small, regular ways to care for yourself, and that's going to look different in every season.

Mental Health and Emotions

Mental and emotional health is a complex subject, and we can't explore all it takes to find wholeness. We need a comprehensive approach, from counselors to medications to diet and exercise and so much more. Sometimes, though, renewing our mental and emotional health can be as simple as creating meaningful rhythms for each day, especially when you find yourself in a season of disruption or in the liminal space between seasons.

Recently Glenn was talking with a friend who had just graduated from college and was planning to attend grad school. During this season, his friend was in a funk. It didn't make sense to look for a job if he was going to grad school, but he hadn't yet applied to any programs. He couldn't seem to shake feelings of sluggishness and a lack of motivation. Glenn wondered if perhaps the surge of adrenaline and dopamine he'd felt at graduation had diminished, leaving him feeling low following the high of accomplishment. Glenn suggested he create some self-imposed structure in his life, like a morning walk routine and a list of chores to do each day. The sudden change from the structure of school life to an unstructured, amorphous glob of time is a disorienting experience we see in our kids every summer! As it turned out, those simple practices picked up the young man's mood and helped him regain his motivation. He went on to complete a master's program and is headed for great things.

Tending to our inner world—our souls—by paying attention to our emotions is vital not just for our mental health but for our renewal as well. One of the things I noticed about Glenn when we first met was his ability to ask great questions, and not just the "What did you do today?" kind. His questions would encourage me to reflect deeply on ideas while considering my feelings and thoughts. I'm incredibly grateful to Glenn for awakening me to a deeper part of myself.

Now I make a daily habit of asking myself, "What am I feeling angry, sad, anxious, or happy about today?"

You likely feel all these emotions at some point on any

given day, but it's easy to blaze through the day or week without even being aware of them. Or when a strong emotion presents itself, you may feel you don't have time to deal with it, so you ignore it and move on to the next item on your to-do list. If identifying your emotions seems difficult, pay attention to your body. Often, anxiety presents itself physically. Do you ever feel your neck or shoulders stiffen, your mind race, your chest tighten, or a knot form in your gut?

Maybe this is a season to pay greater attention to your emotional health. To help you become more aware of your feelings, or any unprocessed grief, you may want to read some books on the subject, carve out time with a trusted friend, or talk with a counselor. In some cases, medication is needed to give us the help we need. There's no shame in any of it.

Some of us need to think about play and recreation. "Working" on our mental and physical health may be far too serious. Perhaps taking up a hobby that gets us outside or with friends, laughing and carefree, is exactly the thing we need. We live in a state where people are always hiking or climbing or fishing or camping. That may be what renewing your body and mind looks like for you.

QUESTIONS FOR TAKING CARE OF YOUR MENTAL AND PHYSICAL HEALTH

- What physical exercise could you do consistently? How much time could you realistically devote to exercise in a week? (Even five minutes a day can help you feel better!)

- What nutritional changes would help you care better for your body? (For example, drinking more water, eating more vegetables and less sugar, or taking more supplements.)

- What types of activities help you stay in a good mental state? Could you schedule time even once a quarter to meet with a counselor or spiritual director who can help you pay attention to your soul?

- What habits do you need to curb or stop so your life has more balance? (For example, cutting back on your consumption of social media or Netflix or alcohol.)

- Where can you work in more play or recreation? How can physical and mental health become more life-giving and fun?

READING FOR RENEWAL

GLENN

I used to carry a book with me everywhere I went. I don't mean as a nerdy kid whose nose was always buried in the pages of some fantasy novel. I mean as an adult. When I first began working at New Life Church, I was an intern in the worship ministry. The team was known at the time for its long meetings that would drift from the strategic to the operational, from high-flying philosophical conversations to quotidian details of scheduling dates and times in the calendar. Often, these meetings would take place over a meal and last for hours. So, naturally, I brought a book. When the topic would drift beyond my interest or to an area that didn't relate to me, I pulled out my book and started reading. I chuckle thinking about this more than twenty years later. It is, quite obviously, a rude thing to do and a habit I would certainly correct in anyone on my team. (Truth be told, I think I actually pulled out a book in the middle of a meeting only a handful of times, and I was sorely chided or at least teased for it.)

Reading is a great love of mine, though I am a ponderously slow reader. I like to think I make up for this by remembering what I read, but I'm sure that's not true. Moreover, I'm an incurable reader of nonfiction. Though I've worked my way through a fair share of classic novels and modern hits (like the Harry Potter series, for example), I read about four times as many nonfiction books as fiction. That's because I want to learn. I read to gain insight, knowledge, and wisdom.

As an avid reader, I didn't realize until the last decade or so that much of my reading is actually a kind of practice of renewal. The realization was gradual, with people like Eugene Peterson helping it along. Peterson is best known in most circles as the translator of *The Message* Bible paraphrase, but to those in pastoral ministry, he is the quintessential pastor. Many of his books are about reclaiming the earthy holiness of that vocation. In 2009, during my first sabbatical—a six-week paid leave to rest and be renewed—I read a few of Peterson's books on pastoral ministry. In one particularly strong book called *Working the Angles*, Peterson called pastors back to their posts by outlining the key but hidden dimensions of our work: prayer, Scripture reading, and spiritual direction. When he talked about Scripture reading, he spoke of a listening ear, an attentiveness to words that could best be described as "contemplative exegesis":

> Words are sounds that reveal. Words make stories that shape. Contemplative exegesis means opening our interiors to these revealing sounds and submitting our lives to the story these words tell in order to be shaped by them. This involves a poet's respect for words and a lover's responsiveness to words.[1]

Most of the nonfiction books I read help me hear the Bible in fresh ways. These books draw out breathtaking themes and paint panoramic landscapes of God's saving presence in his world. They help me see the metanarrative of the Bible and the microdetail of artistry and creativity. Some of these books bring clarity and understanding, while others immerse me in the genius of their literary nature.

In another of his books, Peterson talked about blocking out time in his schedule for study, and honoring that time as if it were an appointment with a real person. That's because reading a book by an author you respect is like spending time with that person. It's a way of being mentored and shaped. And, yes, it's a way of being renewed.

The American preacher and revivalist A. W. Tozer

described kneeling in his study with a book open, asking the Holy Spirit to reveal things to him as he read. But as a charismatic-Pentecostal, I was slower to recognize the spiritual value in reading. Our modes of experiencing God's presence are often loud and visible: speaking in tongues, praying and swaying back and forth, shouting and dancing, and more. To be clear: I practice all those things, too, even to this day! There's nothing like engaging the body in worship and prayer in ways that are active and vocal. But no one told me that reading quietly, underlining sentences, and dog-earing pages are also ways of knowing God and loving him with my mind.

Now that I'm aware of it, I approach reading as a practice of renewal. I try to set aside at least thirty minutes every morning—often, it's an hour—and about an hour every night to read. In the morning, I read whichever book is more demanding; in the evening I usually read something more devotional or reflective. (For example: N. T. Wright in the morning; Henri Nouwen in the evening.)

I've learned one important thing about reading for renewal: I can't read only for the purpose of using what I've read. My input needs to exceed my output. And I don't just mean in terms of quantity. In fact, more often than not, I spend more hours each week teaching or leading up front than reading. But what I take in must always be *qualitatively* better. Let me explain. I'm a pastor who speaks and teaches often. If I want to improve the quality of my content, I need the quality of what I'm reading to be even higher.

Let's pretend that we can assign numeric values to this sort of thing. If I want to preach and teach at an 8, I need to read at a 10. Why? Because something is always lost in the process of input converting to output. To put it a different way, if I want to write like C. S. Lewis, I can't just read C. S. Lewis; I need to read what Lewis read—the works of Saint Augustine, for example. If I want to think like Eugene Peterson, I need to read the writings of Karl Barth—a Swiss theologian whose works Peterson made a point of reading regularly.

Whatever your profession, if you know where you want to be in terms of growth, think of a person who represents that kind of character and life. Then look at the sources that person values, the people whose writings they read and absorb. Maybe you think about leadership or entrepreneurial skills in your line of work, or maybe you're an artist who wants to be inspired or learn how to harness your creativity. It's great to read the writings of the people you admire in your field, but it's even better to read what they read. An easy way to do this is to scan the endnotes or bibliography of a nonfiction book you love. For fiction, it may be trickier because you'd have to find out who inspired the author.

Reading becomes a practice of renewal when we're careful about whose books we're reading, contemplative about how we read, and consistent about when we read. If Sabbath is about stopping, study is about soaking. Both provide perspective beyond the monotonous march of time. With Sabbath, we step back. With study, we step into another world.

SUGGESTIONS FOR ENRICHING YOUR READING EXPERIENCE

- Ask the Lord if there's a particular theme or topic you should focus on for a season.

- Consider choosing a handful of authors whose thinking you want to immerse yourself in for a while. Sometimes certain authors make good pairings, such as Eugene Peterson and Wendell Berry.

- Take notes as you read; for example, jot down key ideas in a journal or make a bullet-point summary of each chapter. Note-taking has been one of the best ways to remember what I've learned and reflect on it in my own words.

- Mix in some fiction and narrative books like biographies and histories to shift your brain into a different mode.

EXPRESSING GRATITUDE

HOLLY

I've mentioned before that I've been in a season of pursuing wholeness and wellness with more diligence and focus. Over the years I've had recurrent, excruciating stomachaches with no clear diagnosis, and they've become more frequent. The frequency and intensity of the pain has propelled me to pursue health in a greater way. I've had a fairly restricted diet for years, and now I've removed sugar entirely. But the most difficult step was . . . no more coffee. Ugghh, that's been painful.

When I removed some of my go-to daily pleasures—coffee and dark chocolate—I noticed myself becoming more irritated over the smallest things. I'm normally pretty steady and calm, but I began to feel unexpected irritation rise up in me. When that happened, I'd want to run to the things that would make me feel instantly better. Since this was no longer a choice, at least for the time being, I had to look the beast in the face. What issues was the Lord asking me to look at more honestly?

Most mornings I get up sometime between five and six o'clock. I started to notice that I was waking up feeling grumpy. One morning I journaled, "5:50 a.m., feeling irritable." Then I paused for a few minutes in silence, breathing deeply and staring out at the mountains. As I entered the practice of prayer, I was tempted to jump ahead and ask the Lord for what I felt I needed in that moment. But I sensed the Lord prompting me to praise him first. Psalm 147:7 (NIV) says, "Sing to the LORD with grateful praise." So I asked instead, *Lord, as I pause to reflect on your grace and goodness in my life, what am I grateful for today?*

In the book *Thanks!: How the New Science of Gratitude Can Make You Happier*, UC Davis psychologist Robert Emmons says that writing short reflections about what we're thankful for—essentially, keeping a gratitude journal—can greatly expand contentment and fulfillment.[2] The research on the positive outcome of practicing gratitude in our lives is compelling. But more importantly, practicing gratitude is an opportunity for us to identify what God is doing in our lives and in the lives of others, and to see how his grace is at work. Gratitude is one way of renewing our hearts each day. It keeps them soft and tender toward the Lord.

God has created our bodies and minds to see more like him when we practice gratitude. Even Jesus thanked the Father regularly. In fact, the Gospels show us Jesus blessing bread—one of the most basic foods—by giving thanks for it. This was, of course, a long-standing Jewish tradition. The Hebrew prayer at mealtime refers to God as the "giver of bread." What else is God the giver of? What other good gifts can we thank him for? Just like with reading the Word or praying every day, it takes discipline to practice gratitude consistently.

IDEAS FOR PRACTICING GRATITUDE

- In a gratitude journal, make a list each day of at least five things you're grateful for.[3] List basic things like sunshine, healthy food, or a home, but include deeper, more personal expressions of gratitude as well.

- Write a gratitude letter to someone who has influenced your life in a positive way, such as a teacher, grandparent, coach, or counselor.

- Go on a gratitude walk around your neighborhood or a local park and tell the Lord the things you're grateful for.

- Send a text or note to someone and share why you're grateful for their presence in your life.

- Pray thankful prayers throughout the day. Stop at lunchtime to thank the Lord for his presence and for how he's working that day.

Of all the things we're intentional about, we easily forget to be intentional about our own renewal. It's also easy to overlook some of the most basic pathways of renewal. For example, you might build a daily walk into your week or set aside thirty minutes every evening to read. Remember, the habits that stick aren't about goals but about an *identity*. So deciding how many books you want to read next year is not really as helpful as you might think. But deciding when and for how long you'll read can be a game changer.

Make a list of some of the ways you experience renewal. Then decide when to test them out, even if it's only for a few weeks. Revisit your list periodically and refine it. This list will be helpful later as you build a schedule for your intentional year.

Being intentional about renewing ourselves physically, mentally, and emotionally is essential. It's difficult to be intentional about anything else if we—our bodies, minds, emotions, and more—are deteriorating and diminishing.

CHAPTER 7

CIRCLES OF RELATIONSHIP

Only those do we call friends to whom we can fearlessly entrust
our heart and all its secrets; those, too, who, in turn,
are bound to us by the same law of faith and security.

Aelred of Rievaulx, *Spiritual Friendship*

GLENN

I sat there, stumped. *What rhythms do I have in my life with friends?* My mind was drawing a blank. While Holly wrote on her worksheet, and dozens of others in the room did the same, I was stunned by my inability to think of where regular time with friends happened in my life.

Sure, there were birthday dinners and occasional get-togethers in each other's homes, but a regular time with friends? I didn't have that.

The longer I sat there unable to complete my worksheet,

the more it dawned on me that I didn't think I *could* have scheduled time with friends. I'm a pastor, after all. I have to be available to people who need me; I have to respond when people ask to meet. And if I'm being proactive, my energy should be directed toward reaching out to key leaders, pillars in our church community, or new believers I want to disciple. I had made a list of older men I wanted to learn from and had been meeting with them with some sort of regularity. But planned, regular time with friends? That wasn't something I thought I could or should have.

Holly and I were attending a conference in Queens, New York, and the worksheet we were filling out was a "rule of life" (we'll unpack this concept in chapter 9). The chart had four squares labeled "prayer," "rest," "relationships," and "work." I had plenty of practices to write down under the sphere of "work," and even under "prayer" and "rest." But the "relation-ships" box had me stumped. With such a busy life and barely enough in the tank for Holly and our children, I wondered how it was even possible to have deep friendships.

Maybe you've wondered the same thing. Your job is demanding. You feel like your time is already stretched to a breaking point. How, in the midst of all you have going on, can you carve out regular time for friendships?

WHAT IS A FRIEND?

HOLLY

It seems like an elementary question. *Everyone* knows what a friend is. A friend is someone you can count on, open up to, share your life with, make memories with, and more. C. S. Lewis described friendship love as being *about* something. It takes a "shoulder to shoulder" posture, with a "common quest or vision" uniting people and serving as "the very medium in which their mutual love and knowledge exist."[1]

But there can be another layer of friendship where the shared bond is an attentiveness to the Spirit's work in each other's lives. As wonderful as it is to have a friend with whom we have a connection or share similar interests, spiritual friends help us pay attention to what God is doing in our lives. Mindy Caliguire made this observation in her book *Spiritual Friendship*:

> When members of the body are meaningfully connected to each other, they feel each other's pain, and they sense each other's joy. And when they are open to it, in a mystical way that is deeply embedded in ordinary human conversation and circumstances, the Spirit of God has unchecked exposure to the soul of each.[2]

When a friend of mine asked if I'd be interested in joining a spiritual-friendship group with her and another friend, I was intrigued. I'd longed for many years to meet with friends more consistently, but it seemed challenging to get something on the calendar and stick to it.

"Tell me more," I said.

"Let's meet once a week with the intention of listening to

one another share about how it is with our souls, praying together, sitting together in silence, and reading a portion of Scripture together," she replied.

It sounded like refreshment to my soul. I said yes.

I've always been intentional about initiating time with friends, but getting up every Friday morning at six thirty for a spiritual-friendship meeting was a new discipline. I'm generally open and honest with friends, but the habit of meeting weekly with this group of friends challenged me to a new and deeper level of authenticity. When I met with someone once a month or every two months, I would tend to give an overview of what had been happening in my life, which is necessary when you're trying to catch someone up. But I noticed that when I met with the spiritual-friendship group, there would often be something more immediate to share— a challenge or celebration. What a joy it was to have these friends as a holy witness to my life in the valleys and on the mountaintops. Sometimes structure in a friendship group feels like it might inhibit connection, but I loved knowing that every week we would have a deep and meaningful spiritual connection because our meetings had a flow, or rhythm. I'm forever grateful for the three years I spent meeting weekly with these dear friends.

Not every friendship has to be a spiritual friendship for us to have deep connections. There are lots of creative ways to have meaningful conversations. In this season, I'm meeting with a couple of friends every other week. Sometimes we read a book that challenges our thinking, and we discuss the ideas.

Other times we share a "soul question" or two ahead of time and come to the group knowing what we'll share. Author and psychiatrist Curt Thompson has four questions he encourages friends to dialogue with each other about:

1. What are you anxious about?
2. What are you ashamed of?
3. What do you want? What are you longing for?
4. What is the next thing you want to create with the Lord?[3]

There are, of course, many more questions to ask, including these:

1. What is the Lord inviting you to say yes to in this season?
2. What are you holding before the Lord with anxiety or fear?
3. What is God asking you to let go of?

Glenn grew up with no brothers, but the Lord always seemed to provide them for him through the church. From his youth-group days to his current ministry, he has found friends who stick closer than brothers. I was always surrounded by friends in my high school years, but I learned to find the right ones in college, the ones who would challenge me and draw out the best in me. Now that Glenn and I are both in church ministry, we've found it difficult to have relationships that are truly mutual rather than one-way, "asymmetrical," or where one of us is the boss, overseer, or pastor. Yet as we work on our emotional and relational health and are intentional in cultivating the right relationships in the right seasons, our friendships have become richer.

THE SPACE BETWEEN

What does it take to have healthy relationships? There is always an unseen and unspoken space between two people. Sometimes it's hesitancy or nervousness. Sometimes it's pain from a previous wound. Sometimes it's bad habits of relating or communication patterns that are destructive or dysfunctional. It could be comparison or competition, feelings of shame or rejection. It could be fear of disappointment. Closing the gap between two lives requires paying attention to our own hearts, moving toward each other, being secure in who we are, and appreciating our similarities and differences. In other words, it takes self-awareness, empathy, and differentiation.

Self-Awareness

Growing up, I didn't talk much about my emotions; my style of speaking was mostly narrative. If you asked me how my day was, I would give you the rundown of where I went, who I saw, what the weather was like, and so on. But throughout my undergraduate and graduate education, I was exposed to different ideas about how people process emotions—and how many of us don't actually process them at all but sweep them under the rug instead. I didn't intentionally stuff my emotions, but I didn't know how to intentionally access them on a regular basis either.

Over the course of many years, I've been exposed to psychologists and counselors and pastors who've helped me understand self-awareness as the ability to recognize our emotions and thought processes and how they affect others. Many of us believe we're self-aware, but often we don't take the time to process our emotions and look at parts of ourselves that might cause us to feel ashamed.

There are many assessment tools—from the Myers-Briggs personality inventory to the Enneagram—that can help us become aware not only of our emotions but also of our preferences and motivations. In fact, I suspect that one of the reasons the Enneagram has become so popular is that it gives us a language we can use to explain why we do the things we do. It leads us on a journey of self-discovery. Glenn is fond of saying that even if the Enneagram is not *ontologically true* (i.e., it doesn't make a definitive statement about the reality of who we are), it is *existentially helpful* (i.e., the experience of exploring which number we identify with is useful in learning about ourselves).

Pete Scazzero, in his Emotionally Healthy Discipleship Course, has popularized a tool from family systems theory called a *genogram* that guides you in mapping out your family tree and outlining key events that shaped your family. One of the goals of tracing the contours of our individual stories is to recognize the scripts we tend to live out. For example, because of my family story, I tended to internalize the script that I needed to stay steady and not show too much emotion.

No matter which self-awareness tools you use, the work of becoming self-aware is a precursor to healthy relationships. It's challenging to have healthy relationships with those who aren't willing or don't have the skills to honestly look at themselves. Our expectations of relationships will vary depending on whether the people in our lives are pursuing self-awareness and emotional health. But even if they aren't, we can always do the work to better prepare ourselves for healthy relationships.

QUESTIONS TO PROMOTE SELF-AWARENESS

Journal your responses to these questions or verbally process with someone.

- What are you angry about?
- What are you sad about?
- What are you happy about?
- What are you anxious about?

Empathy

Empathy is the ability to walk in another person's shoes—to share what someone else is feeling or experiencing. I've had the privilege of walking alongside many people through situations I've never encountered. Yes, I can't truly understand what it's like to grow up in an abusive home or to lose a child to cancer or to be cut off from my extended family. And yet I can offer empathy. I know what it's like to feel anger when I've been blocked from something I hoped for. I know what it's like to feel sadness when a relationship is broken, with little to no hope of repair. I believe it's possible for us to tap into our own stories to enter into the difficult feelings of others.

Empathizing with others comes naturally for some of us; we easily feel what they feel. Others may want to empathize but have a difficult time stepping into someone else's situation, especially without a frame of reference. If you identify with struggling to empathize, try being curious about someone else's situation. Ask questions that can help you see things from their perspective. Offer a nonjudgmental presence. You might be surprised at how even little steps in another's direction will foster a connection.

Differentiation

One of the most powerful concepts that has helped me understand myself is differentiation, a term coined by Dr. Murray Bowen, who developed the Bowen family systems theory. Differentiation is the ability to have and state my own values and opinions while still remaining connected to others relationally. In the middle of the spectrum is healthy differentiation from others, and at either end is an unhealthy style of relating. On one end is being *enmeshed* with family members or other people in our lives. Examples of enmeshment include identifying with our families of origin to the point of not feeling acceptable to them if we live in another town, choose a different career path from the one our parents wanted for us, affiliate with a different political party, or choose not to come to a Christmas gathering. On the other end of the spectrum is being *detached* from our families or other people. Detachment means being so disconnected from others that they no longer affect us. Let's say that your mom expresses anxiety about your moving overseas. If you're detached, you probably couldn't care less about how she feels. You're going to do what you want, no matter what anyone says.

The goal is to work toward differentiation. We'll never be fully differentiated, but we can pursue healthy relationships with others by learning to express our own values and opinions and respect differences.

QUESTIONS TO DISCERN WHERE YOU ARE ON THE DIFFERENTIATION SPECTRUM

- Can I remain myself as I move toward another person to understand their perspective and emotions?

- Can I allow another person's experience of a situation to move me but not diminish my own experience of that situation?

- Do I allow myself to think or feel differently about things than the people I'm close to?

TRUST, TENSION, AND TRUE INTIMACY

GLENN

It's been said that trust is the result of a risk survived.

One of the biggest traps in any relationship is rushing to resolve a conflict and missing the opportunity for intimacy. When we experience frustration, there is usually a longing, a fear, a sadness, or a pain animating it deep beneath the surface. Ideally we would, in the course of growing in self-awareness and relational health, be able to name these deeper feelings and share them with our friends or our spouses. But more often than not, we don't realize what's there until it gets poked—like a dog sleeping under the coffee table.

Early in our marriage, I would want to talk about an issue in the moment, even if it meant staying up way too late. Holly was smart enough to know that if we kept going, tiredness and anger would get the best of us. I finally learned to trust the strength of her love and commitment to return to the matter the next day. The benefit of hitting the pause button was that it gave me a chance to pray about the issue and listen to the Holy Spirit as he searched my heart and uncovered the deeper longing, fear, sadness, or pain. When we returned to the conversation, I was better able to say why the issue mattered to me and how her words or actions were affecting me. We were able to work our way toward a resolution—such as an apology, a new course of action, or a different system for meal planning or putting the kids to bed—but more importantly, we gained real intimacy.

You see, we each have a deep treasure chest of longings

and fears and sorrows and pain, and these manifest themselves as expectations, often subconscious ones. A husband's fear of abandonment might lead to the expectation that his wife should always reply to his texts or take his calls when he is away on a trip. A friend's prior pain of exclusion—perhaps from high school or college—might lead to expecting an invitation anytime a group of friends gets together. A mother's sorrow over knowing that her teenager will be leaving home soon may lead to the expectation that her son shouldn't rush off to his room after dinner. And on it goes.

Once an expectation takes shape in our minds, there are really only two options for what will happen—it will be met or it won't. But here's the funny thing about expectations: When they're met, the person on the other end gets nothing. I mean, it's like paying a bill; we're just paying what we owe. No one gets a thank-you card from their cell-phone company for sending in their payment. So when a friend or a spouse, a parent or a child does what you expect them to do, it doesn't even register on your radar, does it?

But when they don't? Uh-oh. That's when you know. The little irritation you feel that leaks out in a sideways comment or a sarcastic remark, the moody silence you slip into, the temptation to "ghost" them on the text thread—all are dashboard indicators that something is sparking beneath the surface.

But there's hope. You can work your way backward and search your soul with the Spirit's help. Pray Psalm 139: "Search me, God, and know my heart; test me and know my anxious thoughts. See if there is any offensive way in me, and lead me in the way everlasting" (verses 23-24, NIV). Ask the Holy Spirit to reveal not just any "offensive way" in you but also any hidden reasons for your reaction to an unmet expectation. Then express what the Spirit shows you to the person you're in relationship with. (Holly might say, "I think I get irritated when you turn the TV on to check the score because I long for the kind of home where we're present to each other.")

The next risky step to take is turning that longing, fear, sadness, or pain into a request.

"Would it be okay if . . . ?"

"Could we find another way to . . . ?"

"Is there a possibility you might . . . ?"

Requests are the proof of a relationship. When the psalmists brought their petitions to God, they were revealing their confidence in the character of God and the covenant he made with them. Bound up in the act of asking is the belief that God is sovereign and good, and that he is *their* God. A similar thing happens when you're intentional about making a request. Asking demonstrates confidence in the relationship, trust in the other person's character, and a belief that they care about you.

This opens the door to some very different possible outcomes. If the person says yes to your request, then you can express gratitude. (Contrast this with the sense that a met expectation is merely fulfilling an obligation.) If the person says no or that they would love to say yes but feel unable to, then you can return to God as your ultimate source. And if they say yes but struggle to come through, well, that's just an opportunity to take up your cross and deny yourself. I say this a bit tongue in cheek, but it really is important not to put the cross at the beginning of the process by thinking that denying yourself means never allowing the Spirit to search your heart and mine out your longings, fears, sorrows, and pain. That work is essential to becoming a good friend and cultivating healthy relationships.

Each step requires intentionality. Intimacy always does.

Of course, we can't do this much work in every relationship. As much as we would like to, we can't give equal time and attention to all the relationships in our lives. Each of us has a limited relational capacity—which is why we need to be intentional about which relationships to invest in during a given season or year.

CONCENTRIC CIRCLES

How do we know which relationships to prioritize? What would that even look like?

That day in Queens when I couldn't complete the worksheet question about regular time with friends, I realized I had been passive about my relationships. I would respond only when people emailed me to request a meeting or invited our family over to dinner. As a bit of an introvert, when I hit days off, I wanted to crawl under a blanket and read for an hour.

When Holly and I started doing our retreat each year, we began to incorporate a time of praying and talking about which relationships the Lord might be leading us to invest in more. To help us identify these investments, we look at our relationships in terms of concentric circles of increasing size.

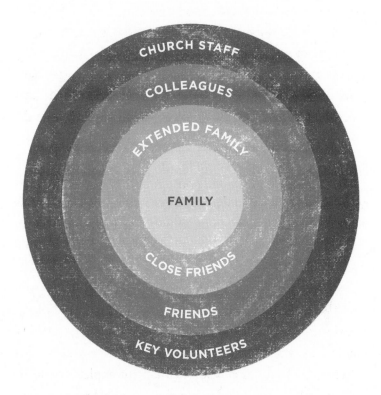

The smallest circle in the center represents family, and the next circle usually represents extended family and close friends. As we move farther out from the center, another circle is for friends and colleagues (though there is some overlap with the close-friends circle). Next is a circle for staff or key volunteers in the church. To be clear, we're talking here about relational investment outside our nine-to-five workdays and ministries, not about the people we have appointments with during the day, anyone from the church who needs help, and those we're discipling on a regular basis.

Once we've sketched out these circles, we then discuss ways we can connect with the people in our lives. Connecting includes things like dates with each other, one-on-one time with the kids, monthly meal groups, quarterly retreat days with friends, overnights with each other, vacations with the family, and more.

It's easy to feel guilty about categorizing relationships in this way. But keep in mind that even Jesus had three disciples who were closest to him, twelve who went everywhere with him, and larger groups who followed him around—not to mention crowds of people he taught, fed, and healed. Paul had relationships that were life-giving to him as well. The names he often included near the end of his letters—you know, the lists we tend to skip!—give us a glimpse of the people in his life. There are no lone rangers for God. And there is no evenhanded way to be there for everyone. In fact, trying to do so ultimately leaves us absent from everyone.

It's also helpful to remember that the whole point of praying through our relational investments once or twice a year is that there are different seasons for cultivating or investing in different relationships.

Holly and I have been blessed to live and work with friends we've known for more than twenty years. This is a gift not to be squandered. But it's hard to schedule time with everyone, especially having four kids who are all pretty active in dance, musical theater, and sports. Most evenings we're just shuttling kids around for hours. Seriously. Not an exaggeration.

Since our time and energy are limited, we've found it helpful when praying about our relational investments to ask the Lord which relationships we should *lean into*, which we should *let lie*, and which we should *let go of*.

LEAN IN, LET LIE, LET GO

HOLLY

The relationships we choose to lean into are the ones that not only matter most—family and close friends—but also have time-bound priorities. For example, Glenn and I are mindful that our teenagers have only a few more years left in our home, so they're at the top of our list.

The relationships you decide to let lie aren't ones to ignore. Letting them lie simply means that if you get together with these people a handful of times a year, it would be just fine. They're important to you, but not your top priority.

The relationships you need to let go of are much harder to talk about. Often these relationships feel one-sided, where you're doing all the work and these friends don't seem to care. It's important, though, to talk about it before silently writing them off! You could say something like "Hey, I sometimes feel that you wouldn't care if I stopped initiating things with you. Is that an accurate picture?" I've learned this often surprises people. Not everyone is an initiator. If a friend indicates they would care, that's a sign they value the relationship. Sometimes all that is needed is a clarifying conversation.

The other "let go" relationships are unhealthy ones that drain you not because these people need something from you but because they don't know how to give and receive love. Many of us are awkward in relationships. But some people are toxic. They're constantly griping about other people, leaking out their pain and hurt, trying to build alliances and take sides, driving a wedge between a group of friends or even in the church. These are the relationships to let go of.

QUESTIONS FOR REFLECTION

- Who helps you pay attention to God's work in your life?

- Which friends walk with you, challenge you, and encourage you? How can you make more room for them?

- How can you become a better friend or bridge the gap between you and someone you want a closer relationship with?

- Which relationships do you need to let go of or pull away from?

- Which relationships do you need to let lie for a season?

- Which relationships do you sense the Lord prompting you to lean into this year?

- What would it take to lean into these relationships?

Reflect on these questions to get a sense of the landscape of your relationships. It might be helpful to start by listing all the people in your life—from home to work to school to church and so on—and then group them in concentric circles. Think about what being intentional with the relationships in each circle might look like. It doesn't have to be hard. In fact, it's likely you already do many things to nurture these relationships. Being intentional about who we are, how we relate to others, and which relationships we lean into, let lie, and let go of is a natural part of cultivating friendships. So why wouldn't we reflect on these things? After all, relationships are the true riches of life.

GREENHOUSE OF GROWTH

GLENN

Throughout this book we've been talking about intentional practices that help us abide in Christ—not only to enhance our joyful union and intimacy with him, but also so that he can produce fruit in us for God's glory and for the sake of the world. Circles of relationship are certainly a key part of cultivating our relationship with the Lord, but they function in another way as well.

Relationships are a greenhouse for growth. In the context of intentional community, we have opportunities to cultivate and evaluate the fruit of the Spirit in our lives. Let me explain. Think of the fruit of *patience*. How do you know the Holy Spirit is producing patience in your life if you are never in situations that require it? When you live with relational intentionality, you will have a mix of symmetrical and asymmetrical relationships. Some relationships will be mutual, and others will be more one-sided. If you're a parent, your relationships with your children may be intentional, but they will never be mutual. Ideally, parents love, give to, and serve their children more than their children could ever do in return. That's how it should be. But relationships that flow more in one direction tend to be costlier. And they require more patience.

Even among friends where relationships are mutual by definition, we need patience. And forgiveness. And gentleness. And faithfulness. This fruit develops only in the context of community. Relationships not only reveal our need for the fruit of the Spirit, but they also become an essential part of the ecosystem in which his fruit grows in our lives.

That's why being intentional with relationships matters so much. If you are laissez-faire in your relationships, thinking, *Whatever will be will be*, you will walk away when a relationship becomes strained or difficult. But that's often precisely the moment when the Holy Spirit wants to drive your roots deeper and push fruit outward in your life. Don't quit. You won't want to miss the moment or the fruit!

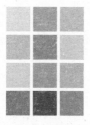

CHAPTER 8

HABITS OF WORK

The only Christian work is good work well done.

Dorothy L. Sayers, "Why Work?"

HOLLY

My introduction to work was watching my dad on the farm. He never seemed to stop. He was always outside doing chores, baling hay, tending to the livestock, or chopping wood for the winter. It seemed like we could never leave the farm for more than a day or two, because something always needed his attention. It wasn't until I was older that I realized how much my dad loved farming. Over the years he told us that farming is a way of life, not simply a way of making money. He bemoaned the agribusinesses that buy family farms, lease expensive GPS tractors, and make it their primary goal to squeeze out as much profit as possible. He would refer to them as "ghost farmers"—the town knew they existed, but no one ever saw them very much, since a lot of the work was done at night with automated machines. I knew that working on a farm wasn't my future, but I'm grateful for the way my dad modeled a different approach to work. He always said he farmed because he loved the land and the livestock. It wasn't a business to him; it was a calling.

At an early age, we learn that grown-ups work. We start to imagine what our work will be, and we gain a vision for what good work looks like in these formative years. But what we rarely talk about explicitly is *why* we work. Whenever Glenn or I head out to a meeting or an appointment or simply open a laptop to reply to emails, our youngest child will sometimes ask, "Why do you have to work?"

It's a good question, and to be honest, there are days when I wish we didn't have to work. But for many Americans, work is a necessary evil, a means to an end. We have to work to provide for our families, secure a good future for our children, and afford the comforts we enjoy or the vacations we love. Once in a while we recognize the madness of the cycle. If we're working simply to take more incredible vacations, would we need them if we weren't working ourselves to the bone? The harder we work, the more escapes we need, and the more escapes we need, the more money we need to earn—and thus the harder we work.

But is work simply about provision? If you and your family had more than enough money for all you could possibly want or need, would you still work? What if work isn't so much about provision but about *purpose*? Why *do* we work?

It may seem a bit strange to talk about work in a book about intentional rhythms. After all, many of us can't do anything about the jobs we have. Our jobs are our jobs, and we need to keep them to take care of our bills and families. Most of us aren't in charge of the companies or ministries we work for. And some of us work really hard, but not at the sorts of things that pay money. You might be a parent who stays home taking care of your children, or you might be in your retirement years with your work life behind you.

God created us to act with purpose in the world. And because of that, the way we work and the way we think about work have deep implications for our spiritual lives. The truth is, all of us can adjust the way we think about work. Our goal in this chapter is to help you reflect on why you work, what work you choose to do, and how you go about it.

We'll start by exploring what the Bible tells us about work. Then we'll discuss what it looks like to discern our own contributions to God's world. Next, we'll explore the differences between a vocation and an occupation and unpack the ways a consistent calling can be manifested in diverse careers. Finally, we'll look at our approach to work and see how we might become more intentional in it.

THE CALLING TO WORK

GLENN

Work wasn't the result of the Fall. It isn't a consequence of our sin or punishment for it. Sometimes we might subconsciously imagine that God, like a parent, said to Adam and Eve, "Ah, see what you've done? Well, since you've disobeyed me, I'm going to put you to work. You're going to pay for your wrongs. It's not going to be all fun and games. Now you have to do some chores."

Work is actually bound up in the very act of our creation. In Genesis 1:26, God said, "Let us make mankind in our image, in our likeness, so that they may rule" (NIV). Purpose is part of our creational design. But not just any purpose: We are called to rule.

Rule is a funny word. It conjures troubling instances of exploitation and oppression. And the older English word *dominion*, used often in the Genesis account, is not much better. What is all this ruling business about?

In the ancient world, when kings extended their rule, they would set up images of their likeness in far-flung regions so that people who had never seen the king could know what he was like. To take it a step further, the king himself was thought to be the image of a god, a representative of some divine power on the earth. The ancient listeners of the words of Genesis would have recognized two points right away. First, they would have noticed that *this* God—the sole sovereign Creator—made *all* human beings in his image, not just kings. Every human life is intrinsically valuable and purposeful. Second, they would have understood the connection between image and authority. Because humans are made in God's image, we have God's authority. To say it plainly: Humans were created to extend God's wise and loving order into the world. We may not be creators, but we are cultivators and collaborators. We partner with God, participating with him in tending the world so it flourishes as he intended. "Be fruitful and multiply," all creation is told (Genesis 1:22, ESV). And in this, God will be glorified.

That's all well and good, but there's a problem, isn't there? What about human sin? Sin impacted our work. After the Fall, according to Genesis 3:16-19, God told Eve that when she gave birth, she would *labor*—notice that the word choice implies resistance. God told Adam he would toil as he tilled the ground. And the ground itself would work against humans, producing thorns and thistles. Only by the sweat of our brow would work get accomplished. In spite of the Fall, our calling to work does not disappear. But now our efforts are often resisted; our motives are sometimes tainted; our industries are easily twisted. Work becomes labor and toil.

Nevertheless, humans still have a special place in the world. God still calls us to work with him to accomplish his purposes in it. And because of this extraordinary privilege, the people of God, fully aware of the stories of creation and sin in Genesis, praise him:

What are human beings
that you think about them;

> what are human beings
>> that you pay attention to them?
> You've made them only slightly less than divine,
>> crowning them with glory and grandeur.
> You've let them rule over your handiwork,
>> putting everything under their feet.
>
> PSALM 8:4-6

The glory we've been crowned with is the image of God we bear and the authority of God we share. N. T. Wright put it this way:

> God wants his world to be ruled wisely, by humble and obedient humans in every sphere, by people who will rely on God's own judgement and wisdom, and who will implement it in their communities to bring healing and hope to those most in need of it.[1]

Work is a glorious call to collaborate with God in cultivating and caring for his creation. Work, believe it or not, is part of our glory as human beings.

DISCERNING YOUR MISSION

Okay, so work is part of our glory. But how do we know what our work should be? That's not an easy question to answer, especially in a fallen world, a world that is broken. So often, societies are organized in ways that run counter to the design of creation, and we're tempted to decide what our work will be solely based on profits and gain. The flow of work strongly moves in the direction of power and manipulation, where the strong get stronger and the rich get richer. *If you want something, take it. Look for the leverage and use it to your advantage. Put yourself first.* These are the messages—conscious or subconscious—that we hear each day.

The Bible is not unaware of the realities of living in a fallen world. In fact, the Old Testament quickly introduces us to all the ways our glorious call to work gets twisted and tainted. Cain is jealous of the fruit of Abel's work and kills him. Abraham lies to protect his life while endangering his wife's, just (he thinks) to keep his calling intact. Jacob takes advantage of Esau's weariness and hunger from toiling all day and cheats him out of his birthright. Laban tricks Jacob into marrying his daughter Leah and working for seven more years for his daughter Rachel, the prize he really wanted. And then, of course, Pharaoh, a ruler outside the covenant people, enslaved the Hebrews to expand the grandiosity of Egypt.

In the middle of the mess, the Bible introduces us to what Jewish scholars call the Wisdom Tradition, a collection of sayings and stories, poems and proverbs that show how to live faithfully in adverse situations. Wisdom is not a set of rules or a list of commands. It has to be discerned. Begin with a fear of the Lord, a reverence and awe for the Creator and his ways, and then set out with trusted advisers and loyal friends to discern what wisdom looks like.

If we were to attempt to distill the Bible's wisdom about discerning our mission down to one phrase—a risky and ambitious endeavor!—we might say something like this: *Our mission is found at the intersection of God's glory, the world's good, and our joy.*

God's Glory

The first element of our mission, God's glory, is foundational. Not only is our work *our* glory, but it is meant to result in *God's* glory. N. T. Wright often uses the metaphor of an "angled mirror" to describe the human vocation. We are "designed to reflect creation's praise [upward] to the creator and the creator's wisdom [downward] into his creation."[2]

Scripture frames this reality another way. Humans have a royal vocation as God's image bearers, but the Genesis creation story also borrows imagery from temple stories. The creation account is like the story of a temple being built. In the Bible, the cosmos was created as a divine dwelling place. Even the language about God resting on the seventh day (see Genesis 2:2) foreshadows what happened when the Temple construction was finished and the glory of God *rested* on the people at its dedication. So humans have a priestly vocation as well. And, God's Word tells us, these twin vocations are renewed in Jesus:

> You are a chosen race, a royal priesthood, a holy
> nation, a people who are God's own possession. You
> have become this people so that you may speak of
> the wonderful acts of the one who called you out of
> darkness into his amazing light.
>
> I PETER 2:9

To the one who loves us and freed us from our sins
by his blood, who made us a kingdom, priests to his
God and Father—to him be glory and power forever
and always. Amen.

REVELATION 1:5-6

"You made [your called-out ones from every tribe,
language, people, and nation] a kingdom and priests
to our God, and they will rule on earth."

REVELATION 5:10

As image bearers of God, we are called to be royal priests,
or angled mirrors who reflect his rule downward and creation's praise upward.

The World's Good

The second element of our mission is the world's good. Too
often we begin our vocational discernment—our search
for what we are called to be—by asking ourselves what
our dreams are. Dreams are good, but the call of God is
sometimes a burden we feel in our bones. Moses was angry
when he saw the Egyptians beating the Hebrews (see Exodus
2:11-12). Nehemiah wept when he heard about the ruined
walls of Jerusalem (see Nehemiah 1:3-4). And we feel a
heaviness when we're confronted with the brokenness of our
world. The wisdom Holly gained through her own journey
toward emotional health inspired her to get her master's
degree in counseling so that she could help others find light

and healing too. I wanted to help worship ministries experience renewal and revival, so I began conducting worship workshops in high school for small churches in rural areas of Malaysia.

Beginning with a burden means diagnosing what's wrong in the world and asking God how we might bring healing. In a sense, all Christians are called to be healers in a broken world. N. T. Wright puts it this way:

We need Christian people to work as healers: as healing judges and prison staff, as healing teachers and administrators, as healing shopkeepers and bankers, as healing musicians and artists, as healing writers and scientists, as healing diplomats and politicians. We need people who will hold on to Christ firmly with one hand and reach out the other, with wit and skill and cheerfulness, with compassion and sorrow and tenderness, to the places where our world is in pain. We need people who will use all their God-given skills . . . to analyse where things have gone wrong, to come to the place of pain, and to hold over the wound the only medicine which will really heal, which is the love of Christ made incarnate once more, the strange love of God turned into your flesh and mine, your smile and mine, your tears and mine, your patient analysis and mine, your frustration and mine, your joy and mine.[3]

That's beautiful, isn't it? Our work is meant to be good news for the world because of the way it carries healing and hope.

Our Joy

Finally, our mission becomes clear through the lens of our joy. What makes you come alive? What are the gifts and talents God has placed in you? What things get you excited?

When I was about to graduate from high school, a close family friend, who was a wealthy businessman, offered to pay for me to become a doctor. He said he would pay for my undergrad degree, medical school, and even training in a specialty area. His only requirement was that I return to Malaysia and help operate a hospital that he would build and start. It all sounded too good to be true. A world-class education paid for, and a career path laid out for me? Talk about a calling as a healer!

There was just one problem. I couldn't stand the sight of blood. I took twenty-four hours to pray about it, since it wasn't the type of offer to dismiss or decline immediately. But flashbacks of watching *ER* episodes on TV confirmed that the medical profession was not for me!

You see, it's not enough to acknowledge that a particular mission or vocation would bring glory to God and good to the world. One of the ways to discern your specific calling is to ask yourself if it brings you joy. The God who knit you together gave you talents and gifts and allowed your life experiences to shape your passions, so when you discover something that brings all these together, joy is usually the result. An important part of discernment is seeking the wisdom of your trusted community and listening to your life to glimpse the tapestry and talents, patterns and passions. All these are signs of God at work in your life, revealing what your mission should be.

God's glory. The world's good. Your joy. At the intersection of these three lies your unique calling as the image bearer God designed you to be.

VOCATION VERSUS OCCUPATION

It's worth noting that your calling is not the same as your career. There could be an overlap, of course, but they are distinct. One is an internal sense of mission; the other is an external expression of that drive in specific circumstances. We could extend this further and say that our vocation is not the same thing as our occupation. An occupation, or career, is the kind of work we do; a vocation is the mission, or calling, that drives us to do it. But the truth is, your vocation could take shape in *many* different occupations, paid or unpaid. You can live out a calling regardless of your job.

I was reminded of this a few years ago when I went through the terrifying ordeal with my vocal cords. After I found out that I needed surgery, sadness, fear, isolation, and other emotions I couldn't quite name began to circle over my soul, descending slowly with increasing weight. I decided to email the footage of my examination to a surgeon in Boston. I took a risk even though I felt vulnerable and a little afraid. Later that day, my phone rang. I didn't recognize the number but answered any-way, which was uncharacteristic of me. Instead of stating my name, I simply said, "Hello," which was also uncharacteristic.

The voice on the other end sounded confident. "Hello, this is Dr. Burns. Is this Glenn?"

My heart raced with excitement. "Yes," I replied. "Thank you so much for calling me!"

We talked for fifteen minutes, and in a calm and reassuring voice, Dr. Burns explained everything he would do in surgery. I shared some of my fears about losing my voice and told him I was a pastor who valued the gift of preaching. He reassured me that there was no chance I would never talk again, and only a minor chance that my voice would be raspy after sur-gery. He told me that a successful outcome wasn't simply about using the right specialized laser; it was also about the person using the laser. The path was becoming clear for me. Minutes after I hung up, his assistant called back to pencil a date on the schedule.

When Holly and I met Dr. Burns the day before my sur-gery, he was so kind and gentle. He answered all our ques-tions and explained the next day's procedure. I had walked into his office with mounting anxiety after discovering that because of the COVID-19 pandemic, Holly wouldn't be able to meet me in the recovery room or even stay in the waiting room. I had never had surgery before, and I wasn't prepared for how lonely it would feel to go through it all alone.

As I was wheeled into the operating room the next morn-ing, hearing his voice brought a wave of calm again. I had been reciting Psalm 23 in my heart, praying and trusting the promise of the Lord to be with me and hold me and be the one who would heal me through the hands of the doctors. An hour or so later, when I awoke from the anesthesia, I heard the surgeon's voice telling me all went well. Seconds later, he called Holly. I could hear him describing the operation and how successful it had been. I felt like crying with gratitude.

The following day, Holly went with me for my post-op follow-up with Dr. Burns, who had ordered two full weeks of total silence. I wasn't even allowed to talk during the appointment! After reviewing the examination videos, he showed us a video of the operation itself. It was absolutely remarkable.

Before we left, I typed a note to him on my phone, and he read it aloud. It said, *Thank you. Thank you. Thank you. You are so calm and reassuring. You're like a pastor.*

He chuckled slightly and said, "Well, no one has ever said that before."

But it's true. I saw echoes of my vocation in his occupation. God had given me the gift of seeing my calling in someone else's work.

GOOD WORK DONE WELL

HOLLY

In various seasons of my life, Glenn and I have both had different jobs and roles. Early in our marriage, I worked in the human resources department at our church, keeping employee files in order. Then I began pursuing my master's degree in counseling, leading trauma recovery groups, and meeting young women for discipleship and pastoral care. After having our first child, I decided to make the care and formation of her life—and the lives of our other three children who followed—my main occupation. I homeschooled them, curating an educational plan that integrated a range of primary sources and supplemented certain subjects with online courses. Along the way, I tried my hand at different side jobs, from teaching ballet to toddlers (including our oldest daughter) at a friend's dance studio to being a content contributor on a major motherhood podcast and blog.

When I came back on staff at the church a few years ago, I found myself pulling on all—well, almost all—these different roles. I launched a large discipleship group for moms of young children and began meeting with people in a pastoral counseling context. I led courses on emotionally healthy spirituality and raised up leaders to join in the work.

There was a common thread in most of these roles, and yet each showed a different shade of my calling in its season. In the process of completing my counseling degree, I felt that I wanted to learn about how to support those who wanted to become foster or adoptive parents. I knew little to nothing about this path but decided to seek out a local organization, Catholic Charities, that could help me. It was an incredible year of growth as I walked alongside a couple who wanted to become adoptive parents and a mom who was trying to discern whether she could raise her own child.

In this current season, I sense God calling me to use all he has equipped me with to serve and support my family and those in our church and local community. Some days that might mean homeschooling my kids or sitting with a congregant in a pastoral counseling office, and other days it might mean writing an article to encourage others. When I wake up in the morning, I often pray, *Good morning, Lord. Show me what it looks like to love and serve you today. Help me to be aware of your presence. I don't want to go my own way.*

Glenn has always joked that I'm an "experiential decision maker," which means I have to try something before I know if it's right. But I think that's how discernment works. You don't discover your calling on a solitude retreat and then start applying for jobs as soon as you return home. Instead, you do what is in front of you, taking steps to test and see whether you have, in fact, arrived at the intersection of God's glory, the world's good, and your joy.

Glenn, for example, could not have predicted the role he is in now. Nor did he chart a course to end up here. He began as a worship leader but studied theology as an undergrad. After eight wonderful years serving our church by leading worship for our college ministry and our Sunday services, he took a step toward teaching and preaching. He and the team were asked to lead a Sunday-night service, and he got to shepherd a congregation for the first time. That led to launching our first off-site congregation—New Life Downtown—along with many more exciting adventures.

Each change wasn't necessarily a step up. He wasn't climbing any sort of ladder. He describes it more like clicking the lens of his calling into focus, discovering greater clarity about who he is and the mission God has given him.

Discerning the work that is ours to do happens as we take steps in each season of life. Just as discernment happens in real time, we cannot wait until we're finally living out our callings to begin working faithfully. Too many of us are tempted to give our all once we're doing something we actually care about. But that isn't how spiritual habits work. Discipline and diligence must be practiced at every turn. As Jesus said, "Whoever is faithful with little is also faithful with much" (Luke 16:10).

When I was given the opportunity to contribute to a large motherhood ministry, I would get up early and stay up late writing articles and outlining podcasts. But the truth is, I'd used those same skills and that same diligence in planning books and curriculum for our kids' education—an unpaid job that often seemed to go unnoticed. I had to practice the unseen tasks with faithfulness before I could step into something more public.

It took Glenn and me a while to become intentional with our diligence. We had so much to learn. We had to ask ourselves, "When are we most fruitful—mornings or late at night?" We also had to think not just about time management but about energy management as well. Which tasks cost us energy and which ones conserved it? How could we try—emphasis on *try*—to shape our weeks so that we could budget our energy well? Were we giving our best energy to our most critical work? For example, it was easy for me to get up in the morning and work on kitchen chores or household duties. But I had to learn that my best time to think, read, and write is first thing in the morning. So I began waking up at five thirty, hoping I'd beat my kids to the day. I'd come downstairs, light a candle, make my tea, and read. Glenn had to realize that watching Netflix at night meant he was getting to bed too late, but if he went to sleep earlier, he could wake up earlier to read and pray.

God calls each of us to collaborate with him in cultivating and caring for his creation. That calling is found at the intersection of God's glory, the world's good, and our joy. We can live out our unique callings in many different ways through the experiences, gifts, and passions God has given us. In each season of life, we discern our callings by taking steps of faith and faithfulness, practicing diligence and intentionality. And in the end, what we hope for is that by the grace of God, we will hear the Lord say, "Well done."

QUESTIONS FOR REFLECTION

- How do you think about work? Is it more of a necessary evil or pain, or is it a holy call to join God in cultivating his world? Think of how you feel about work every Monday morning. (Okay, maybe that's not helpful!)

- What drew you to the work you do? Regardless of whether it is paid or unpaid, what is the burden you felt or perhaps still feel when you think deeply about it? How would you describe your burden in your own words?

- Think of how you feel about work at your best moments. What about it brings you joy?

- How does your work reflect these three elements: God's glory, the world's good, and your joy? Which elements, if any, are missing?

- How might God be inviting you to do your work well? In what areas have you been less than faithful in carrying out the work he has entrusted you with? I know this might be a difficult question, but remember that we can freely confess our failures with honesty because God is abounding in mercy.

Now offer God your work and ask his Spirit to fill you with the grace to do it well.

PRAYER FOR VOCATION IN DAILY WORK

Almighty God our heavenly Father, you declare your glory and show forth your handiwork in the heavens and in the earth: Deliver us in our various occupations from the service of self alone, that we may do the work you give us to do in truth and beauty and for the common good; for the sake of him who came among us as one who serves, your Son Jesus Christ our Lord, who lives and reigns with you and the Holy Spirit, one God, for ever and ever. Amen.[4]

PART 3

ACTION

Making It Stick

Hooray! You've done most of the heavy lifting. You've reflected on the past year, marking memorials to God's faithfulness, expressing gratitude, and confessing where you've fallen short; you've looked forward to the season ahead, listening to the Lord and waiting on his direction; and you've taken inventory of five very important spheres of life—prayer, rest, renewal, relationships, and work—and identified simple rhythms and specific practices you want to integrate into your daily life.

Now it's time to bring it all together and make a plan of action for living intentionally and purposefully in the next season of your life. We'll actually develop a plan for each sphere of life. We're going to get specific and practical. We're going to take the guesswork out of it.

These are what you might think of as pregame decisions that will reduce the amount of complexity you have to deal with on a daily basis. There are so many decisions we all have to make each day. Like Steve Jobs choosing not to waste brain power on wardrobe decisions (hence his choice of a black T-shirt or mock turtleneck every day), to live intentionally, we need to make as many pregame decisions as possible, knowing that we'll still need to make some adjustments during the game, so to speak.

Having a plan doesn't mean you're stuck; it just means you're being proactive.

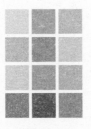

CHAPTER 9

RHYTHMS OF INTENTIONALITY

"Walk with me and work with me—watch how I do it.
Learn the unforced rhythms of grace. I won't lay anything
heavy or ill-fitting on you. Keep company with me and
you'll learn to live freely and lightly."

Jesus, quoted in Matthew 11:29-30, MSG

GLENN

Our kids love LEGO sets. Who am I kidding? *I* love LEGO
sets. When we bought our kids larger sets that had several
bags with the pieces in them—bags that were numbered in
order of assembly—I often did a bit more than supervise the
process. Actually, I might have gotten a little carried away.
Our son wanted to tackle the larger projects himself, so I
decided to let him. It was his X-wing starfighter, after all, not

mine. At first, he made a classic rookie mistake. He opened all the bags and dumped all the pieces out on the carpet—and then opened up the instruction manual. This, of course, made the job much harder, because he had to dig through all the pieces to find the right one instead of focusing on one set of pieces at a time.

Well, we've kind of just done that with this book. Each chapter is like a bag of LEGO pieces, a cluster of practices that help us evaluate the past (chapter 2), prepare for the year or season ahead (chapter 3), cultivate a deep prayer life with God (chapter 4), make room for rest (chapter 5), find places of renewal (chapter 6), invest in relationships (chapter 7), and reframe our work (chapter 8). But how do all these pieces fit together? It can feel overwhelming, like hundreds of LEGO pieces in a pile on the carpet.

As if life isn't chaotic enough, right?

HOLLY

About seven years ago, I was experiencing that kind of jumbled-together chaos. We had a seven-year-old, a five-year-old, a two-year-old, and a baby. One day as I was attempting to read with Sophia while I was nursing Jane (because I couldn't put down a crying baby who always wanted to be held), Norah and Jonas started throwing a ball around the house. I kept saying, "Please stop playing ball in the house. You're going to break something." When they stopped, I continued with Sophia and Jane. Then the next thing I heard was "Mom, can you play a game with us?" So many needs and not enough of me to go around.

In the midst of the daily struggle with kids, I so desperately wanted personal goals or family goals—really, any goals!—to keep me rooted in my relationship with Christ and my relationships with others. I would set goals and try to be intentional and consistent in daily practices, but nothing seemed quite right. My goals were random or disjointed, with no overarching theme or unifying purpose. And I would easily fall short of where I wanted to be.

The problem is, goals are just another way to measure our worth and define our identity. Goal setting often becomes a kind of religion. When we achieve our goals, we feel awesome about ourselves and look down on "lesser beings" who don't read as many books or run as many miles or produce as much content. Or whatever. And when we fail, we're left without any path to redemption. Who atones for you falling off the weight-loss wagon?

Goals are setups for disappointment and discouragement. At best, they're temporary. As soon as you achieve a goal, you stop doing whatever it was that helped you get there. A year after having our second child, I ran a half-marathon. I trained hard for it, running six to eight miles at a time. I flew out to San Francisco with friends, and we made a great memory running the race together. But you know what? I never ran more than one or two miles at a time after that! Habits we establish only to achieve a goal don't ultimately stick.

This was one of the key insights from James Clear's book *Atomic Habits*. For habits to stick, they need to be connected to a sense of identity: *This is who I am.*[1] Runners get out and run because it's who they are, not because they're training for something.

Now that we understand the value of the spheres of life—prayer, rest, renewal, relationships, and work—we need to think about integrating intentional practices into our lives that reflect the season we're in. Which practices do we choose for each sphere of our lives? How do they fit together? And what is the point of it all anyway?

THE RULE OF LIFE

More than a decade ago, when Glenn and I became aware of an ancient practice from Benedictine spirituality called the *rule of life*, or the Rule of Saint Benedict, we realized it was deeper than a set of goals. It was a framework for the spiritual rhythms that characterize our lives. The rule of life is a set of practices that shape us into who God has called us to be. Here's another way to describe it: *The rule of life is a call to order our lives so we may love the Lord and others well.*

The rule of life isn't static. When our kids were much younger, our rule of life included only a few practices because life was more unpredictable in that season. But as the kids have grown, Glenn and I have felt an increasing capacity to put more sustainable practices into place.

Don't be intimidated by the word *rule*. *Rule* comes from

the Latin word *regula*—referring to a standard by which to measure something.[2] Some scholars have pointed out that the word is also related to the Greek word for trellis.[3] A trellis is a structure or framework that supports a grapevine, raising it off the ground and helping it grow upward so it can become fruitful and productive. We all want to be fruitful and productive, right?

Jesus often spoke in agricultural language. In John 15:1-5 (NIV), he said,

> I am the true vine, and my Father is the gardener.
> He cuts off every branch in me that bears no fruit,
> while every branch that does bear fruit he prunes so
> that it will be even more fruitful. . . . Remain in me,
> as I also remain in you. No branch can bear fruit by
> itself; it must remain in the vine. Neither can you
> bear fruit unless you remain in me.
>
> I am the vine; you are the branches. If you remain
> in me and I in you, you will bear much fruit; apart
> from me you can do nothing.

Jesus calls us to abide in him. As we lean into the spheres of prayer, rest, renewal, relationships, and work, we are intentionally shaping our lives to abide in Christ so that we can bear fruit. Developing a rule of life, or a set of spiritual practices, equips us to remain and abide in him. It is an intentional plan to keep God at the center of everything we do.

A rule of life is not a solo project; Christians have been

practicing it for centuries. When we embrace a rule of life, we are joining a great company of Christ followers through-out history. What we learn from them is that a rule of life is meant to be lived out in community. Saint Benedict saw his rule "simply as a handbook to making the very radical demands of the Gospel a practical and therefore an inescapable reality in . . . daily life."[4] The Catholic priest and writer Henri Nouwen said that "a rule offers creative bound-aries within which God's loving presence can be recognized and celebrated."[5]

Still, the word *rule* may be throwing you off. So, at the risk of trying to be too clever with a historic Christian practice, we'd like to suggest thinking of the rule of life as "rhythms of intentionality."

In some way, we already live by a set of practices, or rhythms. You probably follow a general routine throughout your day, even if you haven't intentionally crafted one. But the question is whether our rhythms align with our convic-tions and values. Values should give direction to our daily lives. Unfortunately, all too often our lives don't align with our values. Paying attention to our family rhythms helps me evaluate whether they're reinforcing my values or undermin-ing them. For example, sharing meals together on a con-sistent basis is a value for our family. But many times on our parenting journey, Glenn and I have had to pause and ask if our children's involvement in particular activities fit that family value. Because the schedules for many activities tend to coincide with mealtimes, the answer most often is no.

We've had to be thoughtful and creative in coming up with long-term solutions.

Aligning our lives with our values can be challenging, and there are no easy answers. But without rhythms of intentionality, we can find ourselves adrift in a sea of activities that don't reflect our values as image bearers of God.

START WITH PRAYER

Don't look to others first to decide what your rule of life should look like. Ask the Lord what he has called you to in this season. Rhythms of intentionality help us put God at the center of our lives and seek his calling. God is the Creator, an artist; he will show you what he has called you to put your hands to. Earlier, we used the image of a trellis. Here, it may be helpful to think of these rhythms as stones that build an altar. Each sphere is a stone that makes our whole lives an altar, a way of offering ourselves fully to the Lord in worship.

So, the process of creating rhythms of intentionality must begin with prayer. Glenn and I have found the following prayers helpful in preparing for this creative work.

- *Lord, who are you calling me to be?* As you listen for God's voice during this time, allow him to shine his light on places where you need to grow. This can be a painful process, but it's necessary. So don't rush through it. As you pray, the Lord may bring to mind certain moments and scenes in your life that revealed who you are. You may begin to see yourself honestly for the first time. You will likely find ways of being to affirm—areas of your life that the Lord wants to strengthen and reinforce. And you'll find ways of being to repent of—areas of your life that the Lord wants to change and correct. Ask what it would look like to become more like Jesus in those areas.

- *Lord, what season am I in?* In an earlier chapter, we learned about discerning the seasons of our lives so we might live rightly in them. As you sit before the Lord in prayer, consider these questions: Are there big changes ahead? Have you recently experienced a job transition or crisis in your life? Keep in mind that any significant changes will affect your ability to sustain rhythms of intentionality. What is realistic and sustainable for you in this season? The rhythms you're able to sustain today might not be realistic or sustainable in three or six months. That's why it's important to revisit your seasons regularly and ensure your rhythms reflect the season you're in.

- *Lord, what daily, weekly, monthly, and quarterly rhythms do you have for me?* In a world of crammed schedules, endless to-do lists, long commutes, relational tensions, and constant noise, it's all too easy to live life on autopilot rather than in an intentional way. A typical day in my life looks like this: get up, spend time with the Lord, exercise, make breakfast, help our kids prepare for their days, educate the kids or head to a ministry group or appointment. I have often packed my schedule so full that I'm exhausted by midafternoon. As I began to consider creating rhythms of intentionality, I pondered which practices I wanted to add to my life and which ones I needed to remove. Removing something might mean not doing it anymore, or it might mean delegating it to others to do.

Praying this way is not likely to result in a thundering voice from heaven. But it's a way of surrendering the microdecisions of our lives to the Lord; it's a way of holding it all with an open hand before him. As you bring these questions to God in prayer, you are allowing him to guide your steps and decisions as you consider the rhythms of your life.

CRAFT YOUR RHYTHMS

We've explored how rhythms of intentionality can help us live more freely, peacefully, and purposefully. We've settled ourselves before the Lord in prayer, and we're paying attention to his promptings. Now it's time to do the more detailed work of outlining specific practices to integrate into each sphere of our lives.

It can be helpful to visualize the five spheres of prayer, rest, renewal, relationships, and work as circles with areas that overlap. At the center of these intersecting circles is love: our love for God and our love for others.

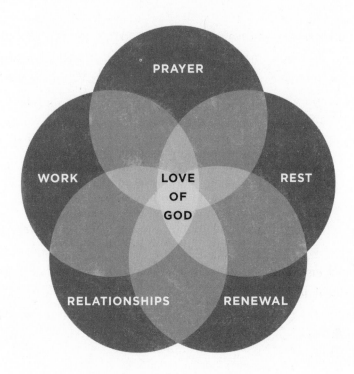

The first three spheres of life—prayer, rest, and renewal—
have to do with our *interior lives*: our communion with God
and the cultivation of our spiritual and physical selves. The
remaining two spheres—relationships and work—represent
our *exterior lives*: the people we're in community with and
what we're called to contribute to the world (our purpose).

As we move through the five spheres systematically, you'll
map out a set of practices, or rhythms, you want to incorporate into each sphere of your life. We recommend adding only one new practice for each sphere at the beginning.
When I first drafted my rhythms of intentionality, I added a

bunch of new practices, felt overwhelmed, and never started many of them. You'll have the best chance of incorporating new practices into your life if you start small and focus on sustaining each practice for thirty or sixty days.

We encourage you to write down the practices you'd like to focus on in each sphere. Take a few minutes to review what you wrote about practices in each sphere in the previous chapters. What stands out? What resonates with you? What does and doesn't feel like the right fit for you and your family? Don't worry about creating a detailed plan just yet— we'll do that in the next chapter. For now, we're simply creating a vision for what we want these rhythms of intentionality to look like.

Rhythms of Prayer

GLENN

Rhythms of prayer and devotion are the practices we covered in chapter 4. They are ways of digging wells to access the living water of the Spirit. You may not need many prayer rhythms, but it's good to have a variety to choose from. When one well seems to run dry, another can connect you to the Spirit in a fresh way.

Thanks to my charismatic background, worship has long been a deep well of life-giving water for me, a rich way of connecting to the Spirit. But years ago, I experienced a season of dry wells, and worship was one of the most significant wells to run dry. By that point, I had spent thousands of hours leading people in worship through music and song.

Our church had released several albums, and some of us were traveling to various conferences and events around the country. I was also part of the Desperation Band, who led worship at youth events and wrote songs that were being sung in other churches. But as I paid attention to my soul during that season, I realized that most of my worship took place on a platform. I also found it difficult to listen to worship music in my personal devotional time with the Lord. Occupational hazard, I guess.

I began to see the flaws in the burgeoning genre of worship music as it became increasingly commercialized and commodified. I also witnessed the tainting influence of the music business and radio hits and became wary of the production values that were creeping into the church.

Some of these concerns may have had legitimacy, but I was missing the heart of the problem: My own devotional life was drying up, and I needed to dig new wells to drink from.

One day as I was reading about Ignatian spirituality, I realized that it had the same heart as the charismatic worship songs I had been raised on. Both practices are about cultivating an abiding presence of God. Both wells access the same water table, the same underground source of God's Spirit. I began to drink deeply from that well and found fresh life.

If we're going to cultivate a deep and vibrant life with God over the long haul, we need a few wells to drink from. Earlier in the book, Holly and I shared some of the prayer practices we've found helpful, such as psalm praying, *lectio divina*, and silence. Now it's time for you to make your own list.

Focus on incorporating two or three prayer practices into your life—a daily practice, a weekly or monthly practice, and perhaps a quarterly practice. For example, before bed each night, I journal the simple version of the prayer of reflection (or Examen) that we walked through in chapter 2. As I prayerfully review the day, I note where I felt joy, angst, sorrow, and guilt. Then I journal a short prayer of repentance for the moments I failed to give and receive love—the things "done" and "left undone," as the prayer of confession says.[6] Finally, I write out a paragraph prayer, asking God for his grace to be faithful and content and grateful. Try it. It may help you sleep better at night!

HOLLY

Another helpful daily prayer practice may be to ask the Lord, *Where have I failed to engage with you today?* One day this past year, my daughter Jane asked me to help her with a math lesson. I was happy to help, but as I sat with her, my focus quickly shifted to the text notifications coming through on my phone.

"Mom, will you focus on this lesson with me?" she asked after I began responding to messages.

In the moment, I knew I should put down my phone and give her my full attention. But it wasn't until later when I prayed, *Lord, where did I fail to engage with you today?* that I realized he wanted me to engage with my daughter over her schoolwork. This simple act in the middle of a normal day was an invitation from the Lord.

It can be hard to see what God is doing or hear what he's saying to me in the moment. But later, when I'm reviewing the day, I find that it's easier to see where he's been at work if I ask him to show me.

For a weekly or monthly prayer practice, think about setting aside a half day for solitude and silence. You might find a quiet old church or retreat center nearby, camp out at a local coffee shop, or take a long walk in a different part of town. In Colorado, where we live, there are a plethora of options, from trails and parks to retreat centers.

For a quarterly prayer practice, think about getting away for an overnight retreat. You could reserve a room at a retreat center or a hotel in town. Leave your phone behind or disable certain apps and email so you can be fully present with the Lord during this prayer time. Bring a book to reflect on, or read through an entire book of the Bible. You'll be amazed at what can happen when you intentionally create space to be with God.

IDEAS FOR PRACTICES OF PRAYER

- Psalm praying
- Bible reading (*lectio divina*)
- A prayer app (like Lectio 365 or Pray as You Go)
- Five minutes of silence and listening each day
- Half a day of solitude each week or month
- An overnight retreat every quarter

Daily

Weekly

Monthly

Quarterly

Rhythms of Rest

Rest doesn't just happen. We have to be intentional about taking a regular Sabbath. When life is overwhelming, we're tempted to just keep pushing through. When is it okay *not* to push yourself? When is it okay to turn off the voice in your head that asks, *What should I be doing right now? How can I make the most of my time?* Believe it or not, you have to think concretely about these things, or meaningful rest won't happen.

As you plan out your rhythms of rest, take the time to think about your sleep schedule as well. How much sleep do you need? What choices do you need to make to get that sleep? What things are impeding good sleep? Are you binge-watching shows at night (ahem, Glenn, are you reading this?) or napping late in the afternoon?

Get specific about times and places and actions and behaviors as you map out what your rhythms of rest will look like.

PRACTICES OF REST

Sabbath

Sleep

Seasons

Rhythms of Renewal

GLENN

What brings life to you? What renews your spirit, mind, and body? How have you "played" in the past? Could you incorporate some of those activities again?

I spent my twenties as a worship leader and then became primarily a preacher-teacher in my thirties and forties. A spiritual director helped me realize that after this shift, I rarely sat at the piano or picked up my guitar. There was no playful space in my life. A few years ago, I began to randomly play the piano in our basement, not to write a worship song, but just to have fun and see what came out. It was renewing.

During the lockdown months of the COVID-19 pandemic, Holly and I started looking for new ways to play as a family. Though we aren't big video-game people, we decided to buy a gaming system. We've had some raucous times of laughter together and loads of fun racing each other in *Mario Kart*. Play is a kind of rest that brings renewal. Think of a recreational activity you could make time for, even if it's only once a month.

When all the kids' activities stopped for the better part of a year, Holly loved the space we had in the evenings to go on walks as a family. Being outside is extremely renewing. Could a morning or evening walk be part of your daily routine? If not daily, maybe once or twice a week, like a walk on a Monday morning and Friday evening as bookends to the week?

In the chapter on renewal, we mentioned gratitude journaling and reading for renewal. How could you build time into your day or week for these practices? Thirty minutes a day for reading or journaling may seem daunting, but what about once a week?

We also mentioned finding a way to check in on your mental and emotional health. Consider reaching out to a counselor or spiritual director and setting up an initial appointment. If your time together goes well, consider meeting on a monthly or quarterly basis as another practice of renewal.

PRACTICES OF RENEWAL

Daily

Weekly

Monthly

Quarterly

Annually

Rhythms of Relationship

Whom would you choose to spend your time with? What relationships are life-giving to you? Who are the people in your life for whom you are irreplaceable?

That last question is always sobering to me. Other people can preach that sermon or teach that text, but only I can be Holly's husband and our children's father and my parent's son and my sister's brother. My most irreplaceable roles are my relational ones, not my functional ones.

So am I giving my best energy to the roles that are irreplaceable?

As you cast a vision for rhythms of intentionality in relationships, you can choose to do exactly that.

- **Begin with the core relationships in your life.** Family usually occupies this central place, the smallest of the concentric circles of relationship we talked about in chapter 7. For those who are single, however, close friends may fill this space. How would you measure your current investment and connection in your closest relationships? Where would you like to grow?

  Holly and I mark out time with each other first. We don't necessarily schedule daily connection moments, but we create the margin for them. One practice we've found helpful is not checking our phones after nine o'clock at night so unhurried conversations can occur. We also look for opportunities to spend an hour together each week, even if it's just grabbing coffee and chatting in the car.

  Similarly, we prioritize individual time with the kids. These days, as our teenagers have more and more activities, car rides are often the most accessible way to spend intentional time together—and that's okay. Don't let an ideal of special dates with your spouse keep you from seizing the moments that are right in front of you—like impromptu late-night chats! Pay attention to the spaces of the day where connection could happen. That might be when some kids are in bed and others are still awake. As you look for moments to connect, don't forget to block out an hour once a month for that special date with your spouse, if possible.

- **Move out from the center to other circles of relationship.** These outer circles include extended family and close friends, casual friends and colleagues, and other kinds of relationships. Who are the people you want to lean into relationship with in this season? How will you do that? Holly and I try to schedule regular meals with friends. In some seasons, we plan dinners every other week; other times, we've found it's best to keep a night of the week open for a spontaneous get-together. Being spontaneous works better for some of our friends whose schedules are less predictable than ours.

  Investment in friends doesn't have to be burdensome or pile endless extra commitments onto your full life. This is where intentionality plays an important role. Sometimes we're only able to connect with friends during our church small-group meetings. At other times, we get together with friends in addition to small group.

- **Identify simple ways to invest in relationships.** At our dinner table, it's not uncommon for us to engage in a lively conversation with our kids. One evening we were playing a round of a family question game. Somehow the question led us into a conversation about love languages from Gary Chapman's book *The Five Love*

Languages.[7] The idea is that each of us has a primary love language or way we feel most loved. Your love language might be affirmation, quality time, gifts, acts of service, or physical touch. Each member of our family took a few minutes to write down their love languages in order from the things that made them feel most loved to what made them feel least loved.

I thought, *Oh, I know what each person will say.* And yes, I did guess some things right, but I was surprised that two of my kids said that gifts were the primary way they felt love. *What?* I mean, I knew they liked gifts—who doesn't?—but this was new information to me. It was also a way Holly and I could periodically bring good to their lives and say "I see you" through a small gift. A gift doesn't have to be expensive. For some of our kids, showing up with a surprise Starbucks drink on a Saturday morning before a musical-theater rehearsal goes a long way.

Extending this principle out, think through the relationships you've chosen to invest in. What are the love languages of the people in your life? What are a few simple ways you could show you love each one in their love language? How could you create a regular pattern to ensure you're meeting them in those ways?

- **Consider specific connection points.** What daily, weekly, monthly, quarterly, and yearly connection points can you build into each of the relationships you've identified? What rhythms of intentionality would reflect the level of connection and investment you've identified for each relationship? Be as specific as possible. Some possibilities might be a daily phone call, a weekly date or coffee catch-up, a monthly meal group, or a quarterly or annual get-together or trip.

PRACTICES OF RELATIONSHIP

Daily

Weekly

Monthly

Quarterly

Annually

Rhythms of Work

Finally, think about the rhythms related to your work, paid or unpaid. We may not think we have much control over how we shape our workweek, but we often have more say in this than we realize. Choosing to be intentional about your rhythms of work impacts a significant chunk of your life.

- **Think about the big picture.** What has God called you to put your hands and feet to in this season? What talents, resources, and gifts has he given you to use for the benefit of others? How can you best use your time? When are you most fruitful in your work?

- **Create achievable, consistent practices.** Whether your work is paid or unpaid, deliberate and thoughtful practices can help you make the most of your time. Scheduling your day or week in chunks of time can often improve focus. For example, to prevent constant interruptions, block off time each day to respond to emails or check social media, such as first thing in the morning, half an hour before lunch, or at the end of the workday. You might also want to designate specific laundry days, yardwork days, and days for projects around the house. In my work, I block off a day for study (reading and writing) and schedule all my pastoral appointments on two afternoons during the week. Creating achievable, consistent work practices sharpens focus and increases productivity because you aren't wasting time and energy figuring out what to do with the little window of time you have. And it's easier on the brain if you don't have to switch modes multiple times a day.

PRACTICES OF WORK

Daily

Weekly

Monthly

Quarterly

Annually

STEPPING INTO YOUR RHYTHMS

HOLLY

Once you complete your rhythms of intentionality, sit with them for a day or a week and ask the Lord to show you if what you've crafted is sustainable. You may decide you need to remove or add certain practices. Maybe you forgot to include a significant part of your life in your plan, and now you need to find space for it.

When I reviewed and revised my rule of life last year, I realized I hadn't created space in my weekly rhythms for family devotions with the kids. We had been consistent for a season, but when life got busy, it dropped out of our routine. Revisiting my rhythms of intentionality gave Glenn and me an opportunity to reevaluate the best time for our family to pursue God together each week.

After you've settled on different rhythms of intentionality for each of the five spheres of life, reread and rethink them on a regular basis. Initially I reviewed my rule of life only once a year. But when I discovered during the first review that I had completely forgotten or abandoned some practices a month or two after creating them, I realized I needed to review my rhythms of intentionality quarterly or biannually at a minimum. Some people post their rule of life in a place they'll see daily as a reminder of the rhythms they want to live out.

You don't have to rigidly adhere to your rule of life. That's why we don't like the word *rule*. It's not a law; it's a set of practices that shape us into who God has called us to be. There's always a tendency to turn rules into ways of impressing God or feeling good about ourselves. So take a deep breath. If you're overwhelmed, set aside your rule of life for a moment; then come back to it later and incorporate just one change for each of the five spheres. The goal of being intentional about the rhythms of our lives is for the Holy Spirit to meet us in those rhythms with freedom, peace, and purpose. As Jesus said, the Sabbath was made for us and not the other way around. This applies to all our other rhythms.

A rule of life is a big-picture vision that takes shape as you fit together the various unassembled LEGO pieces of your life. As every child knows, the fun is in breaking up the pieces and making new things with them. So don't get stuck in one pattern of practices. And don't freeze waiting for the perfect plan to materialize. Good intentions don't make up a life. We have to create ways of turning intentions into actions. We have to choose practices that will make our paths clear.

Speaking of clarity, there's one final piece to this process of creating rhythms of intentionality: the calendar.

CHAPTER 10

CALENDAR RULES

You do not rise to the level of your goals.
You fall to the level of your systems.

James Clear, *Atomic Habits*

HOLLY

Glenn hates it when I say, "Can we go over the calendar?" It always takes longer than I think it will, and he gets impatient while I adjust events in real time. But we still prioritize this task because we both know how awful it is when we forget to put things on the calendar and then realize we've double-booked ourselves! Or we don't know who's going to pick up which kid from which afternoon activity during the school week!

Calendaring is much more than coordinating. When we craft a specific plan and write it down, we're actually embodying our values. You know the saying that a person's bank account reveals what they truly value? (I suppose it's a modern spin on Jesus' words in Matthew 6 about where our treasure lies.) Well, the same could be said about time. What we spend our time on reveals what we value. And conversely, if we value something but don't put it on the calendar, it remains an ambiguous idea—something we want to do but don't actually know when we're going to do.

We've probably all experienced this. We think, *I'd like to start working out*, or *I want to read the Bible more*, or *I want to spend more time with my friends*. But it never happens. Or we start, but other stuff gets in the way, and we don't follow through. The key thing that turns an idea or a desire into a *practice* is knowing when and where we're going to do it.

GLENN

At first glance, this calendar practice may sound overly practical and not sufficiently spiritual. But the details equip us to live out our rhythms of intentionality. Kellogg School of Management professors Loran Nordgren and David Schonthal highlight the difference between "fuel"—motivation, value, reasons—and "friction"—obstacles, ambiguity, effort. Whenever we want to introduce a new behavior or idea, we tend to focus on the fuel.[1] We explain the reasons; we underscore the importance; we do everything we can to persuade people. But that assumes people always choose what they believe is best. This unfortunately isn't true. People often choose what's easiest. And because this is the reality for most of us, we need to reduce the ambiguity about how to act on an idea, as well as the effort required to do so.

So as you're seeking to make rhythms of intentionality stick in your life, think about how you can make it easier. Part of the key to adopting new practices is not just clarifying the why; it's simplifying the how. And the best way to do that is to eliminate the ambiguity around it. If you have to decide every day when and how you're going to read your Bible, as well as which book and how many chapters you want to cover, you'll hardly ever do it. But if you know that shortly after waking up, you're going to sit in your chair and read through the Gospel of John, let's say, then you've made the plan, and the pathway toward adopting this practice will be a little bit easier.

Consider that when Jesus taught his disciples about prayer, he spoke of a specific rhythm and place: "When you pray, go to your room, [and] shut the door" (Matthew 6:6). Calendaring isn't just about setting a time. Place and pathway matter in our formation as well.

In my calendar, it says—and has said this for years now!—that I will pray the Psalms at six o'clock every morning. But can I be honest? I haven't done it regularly for the last couple of years, mostly because my plan is missing a few specifics. When I first started praying the Psalms, I used an Anglican prayer book that included a reflection prayer after each psalm. I sat in the chair in the corner of our bedroom and prayed through this book pretty consistently. But after finishing a few more prayer books, I stalled because I hadn't decided *how* or *where* I was going to pray the Psalms. The chair I'd been using in our bedroom also became less of an option as our kids got older and started filing in and out of our room and bathroom to grab things or talk to Holly or get ready for the day. A lack of specificity about how and where I'm going to pray the Psalms has created obstacles to the practice even though I've always known when I was going to do it.

The calendar is more than a schedule. Think of it as a written record of how you will embody the practice the Spirit is leading you to integrate into your life.

CREATING A PLAN

Calendaring your rhythms of intentionality takes some focus and time on the front end, but eliminating ambiguity up front—by answering questions about each practice, such as where, when, how long, with whom, how often, and more—increases the odds that you'll follow through. Remember, we're not setting goals for the sake of achievement. In fact, we aren't setting goals at all; we're developing intentional practices that reflect and reinforce our identity as beloved children of God and help us grow up in Christ for the glory of the Father and the good of the world. Here are some helpful guidelines as you map out the details of your plan.

- **Find a calendar that works for you.** You might use the calendar on your phone or a handheld written planner. Or maybe you prefer using a big family calendar on the wall. Wherever you jot down your practices, it needs to be something you see and engage with regularly.

- **Revisit the rhythms you mapped out in the last chapter.** As you review each practice, think through the details that will equip you to live it out. Then write these details—days, times, locations, resources—on your calendar.

- **Take advantage of the repeat feature on your phone.** Is the first Friday night of the month the time to invite friends over? Or are you going to work out every Monday, Wednesday, and Friday morning? Schedule it on your phone using the repeat feature. Do you need to block off time for solitude to walk and think and pray? Choose one day a month and set it up on your phone for each month.

Here's the thing: Unless you're intentional about recording practices on your calendar, you'll fool yourself into thinking you have "margin" for all kinds of stuff. You'll say yes to things you shouldn't say yes to or things that you can technically fit in but that end up taking you away from something better. Remember Mary, who chose "the better part" and sat at the feet of Jesus (see Luke 10:38-42)? Schedule first what matters most. When is your time with Jesus? Your time with family? When will you rest and refresh? Eugene Peterson famously scheduled afternoon appointments with "FD" three times a week. During these two-hour meetings, he read the works of Fyodor Dostoyevsky.[2]

You've identified what's most important. Now make space for it. You can't leave the crucial stuff of life for when you have time. You always have time. And you get to choose—within limits—how you spend it.

Be bold. Be specific. Be intentional.

UPDATES

HOLLY

Because our lives are dynamic—with two teenagers, one middle schooler, and a child in elementary school, life moves and changes quickly!—we have to revisit the calendar often. Many of our rhythms remain steady—like working out, praying, and meal-group nights with friends. But other things shift—like when Glenn schedules a day of solitude, or when I grab some time with friends, or when Glenn and I arrange a getaway for the two of us for a couple of nights (which we try to do two or three times a year). Now that we have teens who are driving (pray for us!) and working, their schedules shift from week to week as well.

In this season, our family has a weekly calendar meeting on Sunday nights to make sure we're all on the same page for the week ahead. And I easily spend half an hour each day adjusting and updating the calendar. Much of this involves coordinating calendars and activities. But school and dance and soccer are essentially our kids' rhythms of work, and these rhythms often affect the rhythms of prayer, rest, renewal, and relationships that Glenn and I schedule.

If you're single, whether you live with housemates or not, your schedule can morph around your friends' schedules. The Sabbath day you were hoping to spend at home reading might be the day they want to go out to the movies. So your phone keeps lighting up with texts and invitations to do things, and you can't resist. But there goes your hope of renewing your soul in solitude. Or maybe there isn't much structure in your life because everything continually shifts around and all plans are provisional. If this describes your situation, think of ways to create a self-imposed structure. Honor your time with the Lord or with yourself as an appointment that can't be broken. Revisit the calendar regularly and assess whether your rhythms align with your values. Is your life squeezing out the practices the Spirit wants you to cultivate?

I used to play snare drum in the marching band in high school, and as any musician knows, it's hard to stay in the groove of one rhythm when another rhythm is blaring in your ears. Imagine playing a 4/4 beat while a waltz is blasting on the speakers. The calendar is about figuring out how to turn down the noise, eliminate the distractions, and focus on the things that are most important in this season. It takes consistent tweaking.

From reflecting on the past and praying about the year ahead to asking God to speak a word for the season to identifying intentional practices we need to cultivate a life of prayer, rest, renewal, relationships, and work, it all comes down to time and place and pathway. And it gets enshrined in the calendar.

Write out some specific dates, times, places, and pathways for practices in each sphere of life.

Prayer

Rest

Renewal

Relationships

Work

EPILOGUE

GLENN

Here we are at the end of this book—and the beginning of your intentional year. How do you feel?

If you're overwhelmed, thinking you can't possibly do this, we get it. Often, Holly and I think we can do more than we can, or change things more quickly than we can—and then we learn the hard way that we can't.

So take a deep breath. Welcome the Holy Spirit once again. The Nicene Creed calls the Holy Spirit "the Lord, the giver of life."[1] It's important to note that he is the *giver*, not the one who *gave*. He still gives life. At each moment of each day, the Spirit *gives* life to each one of us.

This life of yours truly comes from God. "You are not your own," as the Scriptures remind us (1 Corinthians 6:19, ESV). God created and redeemed you. He is the one who sustains and empowers you.

Any talk of living intentionally is simply a way of participating in the work of the Father, Son, and Holy Spirit in us and through us. When we live intentionally, we are saying yes to the flood of love the Father has lavished on us, yes to abiding in Jesus, yes to the power and presence of the Holy Spirit. As one man remarked to me after I preached on this, the words "rhythms of intentionality" form the acronym *ROI*, which in the business world stands for "return on investment." He wanted to make the point that there is a return on the investment of being intentional with our lives. True: When we sow to the Spirit, Paul said, we will reap eternal life (Galatians 6:8, ESV).

The harvest is the fruit of the Spirit. Freedom, peace, and purpose come from God and are found in God. They aren't the result of our own cleverness or discipline. He is the source. Rhythms of intentionality are simply ways of taking the posture of the receiver—ways of standing under the waterfall of grace.

But that's not all. It isn't just fruit that results. Do you know one of the other marks of the Spirit's work? Not only does it make our lives look like Jesus and glorify God, but it leads to the good of the church and the world as well. When Paul wrote about the gifts of the Spirit, he spoke of the Spirit leading us to confess Jesus as Lord and empowering us to edify the church.

This means that the intentional year—your intentional life!—is not really about you. It's about how your life becomes good news for the world. The rhythms of prayer, rest, renewal, relationships, and work that you cultivate in your life are meant to produce fruit for the sake of others, gifts for the good of the church and the world. When you're healthy, intentional, and living in freedom, peace, and purpose, others benefit. Yes, Irenaeus was right: The glory of God is the human fully alive. And the good of the world is found when Christians flourish with the fruit and gifts of the Spirit.

So, in the end, it all comes down to love. These rhythms of intentionality are rhythms of love. They move us toward loving God and loving others as we love ourselves. Love is at the burning center of the intentional life. Love is what remains. Love is what the triune God embodies and expresses in essence and relationship. Love is what the Father, Son, and Holy Spirit draw us into.

Our prayer for you is what Paul prayed for the Ephesians:

This is why [we] kneel before the Father. Every ethnic group in heaven or on earth is recognized by him. [We] ask that he will strengthen you in your inner selves from the riches of his glory through the Spirit. [We] ask that Christ will live in your hearts through faith. As a result of having strong roots in love, [we] ask that you'll have the power to grasp love's width and length, height and depth, together with all believers. [We] ask that you'll know the love of Christ that is beyond knowledge so that you will be filled entirely with the fullness of God.

Glory to God, who is able to do far beyond all that we could ask or imagine by his power at work within us; glory to him in the church and in Christ Jesus for all generations, forever and always. Amen.

EPHESIANS 3:14-21

ACKNOWLEDGMENTS

To our kids—You are the people who matter most to us in this world. Pursuing living an intentional life has helped us prioritize spending our days with you in the ordinary and special moments. It's one of our greatest joys to be a witness to your lives and walk alongside you.

To our amazing editor, Caitlyn—*Holly:* You have been a voice in my life encouraging me to write for many years. You've listened to my ideas, invited me to writers' retreats, and believed I could write a book. And now I have the immense privilege of calling you my editor. You're incredible! *Glenn:* You saw the vision of this project and championed it from the start. I'm grateful for the way you came alongside Holly and me, weaving our voices together and helping us learn how to cowrite this book. Your gentle guidance and wise input have been just what we've needed.

To our agent and friend, Alex Field—Thank you for believing in us and championing me (Glenn) for many years. Your enthusiasm about this practice and encouragement to put it to paper for others lit a fire in us.

To our friends (you know who you are)—We don't know where we'd be without you. You've listened to us on our darkest days and walked with us in seasons of joy. *Holly:* You've affirmed me and encouraged me to write, even when I couldn't find my voice. I'm forever grateful to be your friend. *Glenn:* You've helped me give my attention to the right opportunities at the right time, and you've shaped the person that I am.

HOLLY

Mom and Dad—Thank you for your constant presence in my life, and for your listening ears, words of encouragement, and consistent prayers. I wouldn't be where I am today without your love and support.

Abby—God gave me a special gift early in life when he let me be your sister. You are one of the most servant-hearted people I know. You consistently put others first, and I'm lucky to walk through life with you and your family.

Sally Clarkson—You are one of my biggest cheerleaders. You've been encouraging me to share my voice for years. Thank you for giving me opportunities to speak, write, and podcast, and thank you for helping me believe it was possible for me to write a book. It's finally happening!

GLENN

Dad and Mum—Thank you for cultivating habits that have shaped me over the years. Watching you pray, serve, and give has taught me what a flourishing life looks like.

Tracy—My big sister. You were the first to show me what being intentional about friendships looks like. Thank you for your encouragement and excitement, and for the ways you remind me to find the places where we have agency in life.

To the mentors and sages who have helped me think intentionally about being a husband, father, son, and friend—You may not have known what was happening in all those coffee appointments and lunches and walks, but you've guided me along a path that I now hope to illuminate for others.

NOTES

CHAPTER 1: THE SPIRITUALITY OF INTENTIONALITY

1. Allen Iverson, quoted in Jonathan Tannenwald, "Allen Iverson's 'We Talkin' 'bout Practice' Rant Was 15 Years Ago," *Philadelphia Inquirer*, May 5, 2017, https://www.inquirer.com/philly/blogs/sports/sixers/Allen-Iverson-practice-rant-video-Philadelphia-76ers-press-conference.html.

2. Charles Duhigg, *The Power of Habit: Why We Do What We Do in Life and Business* (New York: Random House Trade Paperbacks, 2014), ch. 4.

3. N. T. Wright, *After You Believe: Why Christian Character Matters* (New York: HarperCollins, 2010), 18–21.

4. David Zahl, *Seculosity: How Career, Parenting, Technology, Food, Politics, and Romance Became Our New Religion and What to Do about It* (Minneapolis: Fortress Press, 2019), 4.

5. Dallas Willard, *The Great Omission: Reclaiming Jesus's Essential Teachings on Discipleship* (San Francisco: HarperSanFrancisco, 2006), 166.

CHAPTER 2: REFLECTING ON THE PAST

1. Kyle Strobel and John Coe, *Where Prayer Becomes Real: How Honesty with God Transforms Your Soul* (Grand Rapids: Baker, 2021), 151.

2. *The Book of Common Prayer*, 1979 ed. (New York: Oxford University Press, 2005), 454.

CHAPTER 4: PRACTICES OF PRAYER

1. Henri Nouwen, *In the Name of Jesus: Reflections on Christian Leadership* (New York: Crossroad, 1989), 10–11.
2. Martin Luther, *A Simple Way to Pray* (Louisville, KY: Westminster John Knox, 2000), 18.
3. Russell Moore, *Adopted for Life: The Priority of Adoption for Christian Families and Churches* (Wheaton, IL: Crossway, 2015), 46–47.
4. Pete Greig, *How to Pray: A Simple Guide for Normal People* (Colorado Springs: NavPress, 2019).
5. Eugene H. Peterson, *Eat this Book: A Conversation in the Art of Spiritual Reading* (Grand Rapids: Eerdmans, 2006), 116.

CHAPTER 5: THE POWER OF REST

1. Bryan Lufkin and Jessica Mudditt, "The Case for a Shorter Workweek," Worklife, BBC, August 24, 2021, https://www.bbc.com/worklife/article/20210819-the-case-for-a-shorter-workweek.
2. Lynne M. Baab, "Sabbath Keeping—It's OK to Start Small," accessed March 1, 2022, https://www.lynnebaab.com/articles/sabbath-keepingits-ok-to-start-small-.
3. Ken Shigematsu, *God in My Everything: How an Ancient Rhythm Helps Busy People Enjoy God* (Grand Rapids: Zondervan, 2013), 45.

CHAPTER 6: PATHWAYS OF RENEWAL

1. Eugene H. Peterson, *Working the Angles: The Shape of Pastoral Integrity* (Grand Rapids: Eerdmans, 1987), 117, 125.
2. Robert A. Emmons, *Thanks!: How the New Science of Gratitude Can Make You Happier* (Boston: Houghton Mifflin, 2007), cited in Robert Emmons, "Why Gratitude Is Good," *Greater Good*, November 16, 2010, http://greatergood.berkeley.edu/article/item/why_gratitude_is_good.
3. For other helpful ideas, see Tiffany Musick, "What Good Is Gratitude?: The Role of Thanksgiving in Personal Development," Point Loma Nazarene University, https://www.pointloma.edu/resources/counseling-psychology/what-good-gratitude-role-thanksgiving-personal-development.

CHAPTER 7: CIRCLES OF RELATIONSHIP

1. C. S. Lewis, *The Four Loves* (New York: Harcourt Brace, 1988), 71.
2. Mindy Caliguire, *Spiritual Friendship* (Downers Grove, IL: IVP Connect, 2007), 18.
3. Curt Thompson (presentation, Springs Mental Health Summit, Colorado Springs, November 7, 2020).

CHAPTER 8: HABITS OF WORK

1. N. T. Wright, *Broken Signposts: How Christianity Makes Sense of the World* (New York: HarperOne, 2020), 167.
2. N. T. Wright, *Interpreting Scripture: Essays on the Bible and Hermeneutics* (Grand Rapids: Zondervan Academic, 2020), 264.
3. N. T. Wright, *For All God's Worth: True Worship and the Calling of the Church* (Grand Rapids: Eerdmans, 1997), 101.
4. *The Book of Common Prayer*, 1979 ed. (New York: Oxford University Press, 2005), 261.

CHAPTER 9: RHYTHMS OF INTENTIONALITY

1. James Clear, *Atomic Habits: An Easy and Proven Way to Build Good Habits and Break Bad Ones* (New York: Avery, 2018), 34.
2. Anthony Rich, *The Illustrated Companion to the Latin Dictionary and Greek Lexicon* (London: Longmans, 1849), 547.
3. Ken Shigematsu, *God in My Everything: How an Ancient Rhythm Helps Busy People Enjoy God* (Grand Rapids: Zondervan, 2013), 21.
4. Esther de Waal, *A Life-Giving Way: A Commentary on the Rule of St. Benedict* (London: Continuum, 1995), xi.
5. Henri Nouwen, quoted in Leonard E. Hjalmarson, *An Emerging Dictionary for the Gospel and Culture: A Conversation from Augustine to Žižek* (Eugene, OR: Resource Publications, 2010), 131.
6. *Book of Common Prayer*, 454.
7. Gary Chapman, *The Five Love Languages: The Secret to Love That Lasts* (Chicago: Northfield, 2015).

CHAPTER 10: CALENDAR RULES

1. Loran Nordgren and David Schonthal, *The Human Element: Overcoming the Resistance That Awaits New Ideas* (Hoboken, NJ: John Wiley & Sons, 2021), 2–3.
2. Eugene H. Peterson, *Under the Predictable Plant: An Exploration in Vocational Holiness* (Grand Rapids: Eerdmans, 1992), 49–50.

EPILOGUE

1. *Britannica*, s.v. "Nicene Creed," accessed January 19, 2022, https://www.britannica.com/topic/Nicene-Creed.

NavPress is the book-publishing arm of The Navigators.

Since 1933, The Navigators has helped people around the world bring hope and purpose to others in college campuses, local churches, workplaces, neighborhoods, and hard-to-reach places all over the world, face-to-face and person-by-person in an approach we call Life-to-Life® discipleship. We have committed together to know Christ, make Him known, and help others do the same.®

Would you like to join this adventure of discipleship and disciplemaking?

- Take a Digital Discipleship Journey at **navigators.org/disciplemaking**.
- Get more discipleship and disciplemaking content at **thedisciplemaker.org**.
- Find your next book, Bible, or discipleship resource at **navpress.com**.

 @NavPressPublishing

 @NavPress

 @navpressbooks

CP1790